TURNAROUND

*The Remarkable Story of an Institutional
Transformation and the 10 Essential
Principles and Practices that Made It Happen*

JASON K. ALLEN

PUBLISHING
NASHVILLE, TENNESSEE

978-1-5359-4116-7

Published by B&H Publishing Group
Nashville, Tennessee

Dewey Decimal Classification: 303.3
Subject Heading: LEADERSHIP \ ORGANIZATIONAL
CHANGE \ MIDWESTERN BAPTIST
THEOLOGICAL SEMINARY

Unless otherwise noted all Scriptures are taken from the
New American Standard Bible, copyright © 1960, 1971, 1977, 1995,
2020 by The Lockman Foundation. All rights reserved.

Scripture references marked ESV are taken from the English Standard
Version, ESV® Text Edition: 2016. Copyright © 2001 by Crossway
Bibles, a publishing ministry of Good News Publishers.

Scripture references marked KJV are taken from
the King James Version, public domain.

Cover design by Darren Welch. Author photo by
Midwestern Seminary (MBTS) Communications Staff.

2 3 4 5 6 7 8 • 26 25 24 23 22

This book is dedicated, with deep appreciation, to Dr. R. Albert Mohler Jr. Since my college years, he's been a source of support and encouragement. In more recent years, he served as a mentor and one under whom I was privileged to serve. And now, for the past decade, he's been a trusted colleague in this great, noble work of Southern Baptist theological education. In all these stations and in every season of life, he's been and remains a dear friend.

Yet, this book is about leadership. Though our personal relationship merits this dedication, Dr. Mohler's life of leadership almost necessitates it. His leadership at Southern Seminary, to Southern Baptists as a whole, and to the broader evangelical world is as distinct as it is expansive.

Scripture teaches us to give honor to whom honor is due. Thus, I'm delighted to honor Albert Mohler with this dedication.

Acknowledgments

One clear sign of God's favor on my life is the people he's brought into it. Each one of these family members, friends, and colleagues is a tremendous source of blessing, encouragement, and support.

At the personal level, my life and ministry is enabled and enriched by the prayers and encouragement of my family. God has abundantly blessed me with my wife Karen and our children Anne-Marie, Caroline, William, Alden, and Elizabeth, who have surpassed my every hope and dream as to what they'd be and mean to me. They are a constant source of love, joy, and support. We are not a perfect family, but we are a happy one. To my favorite six people on the planet, thank you.

At the institutional level, my colleagues literally made this book possible. The story I tell isn't my story—it's our story. The team God has given to me is second to none. May they find delight in seeing their fingerprints throughout this book, even as I find delight in them.

My office staff, likewise, is an invaluable source of support and encouragement. Most especially, I'm thankful for Tyler Sykora, Dawn Philbrick, Lauren Hanssen, and Ashley Campbell. These people are an absolute delight to serve with, and they go about their daily tasks with graciousness and competence. More broadly, Justin Love provided invaluable research help, as did Russ Meek on the editorial front. Thank you.

Furthermore, I'm thankful to the team at B&H Publishing Group, especially Devin Maddox and Taylor Combs. Thank you, dear friends, for believing in this project and for working with me to bring it to fruition.

Last, and most of all, I'm indebted to my Lord and Savior, Jesus Christ. Like every other ministerial undertaking, none of this would be possible without His grace, calling, and enabling. May this book, and all that I do, bring Him much glory.

Contents

Introduction

I believe that most everything you've learned about leadership is incorrect. And if you are leading as you've learned, you're probably doing it wrong.

I realize this is a controversial way to begin a book, but I believe it is an accurate—and essential—assertion. At least keep open the possibility that you need to *unlearn* a few things about leadership as you read this book.

In fact, in this book I aim to simplify the needlessly complex galaxy of leadership mantras, materials, and theories. In so doing, I hope to lift up and encourage you, the weighed-down leader.

Leading in the twenty-first century is a daunting responsibility. Cultural chaos, demographic change, political polarization, and financial challenges create a forbidding environment for most every leader. These challenges, and more, are probably why you picked up this book.

The leadership industrial complex promises to help you overcome these challenges. It forces its way onto the scene, arguing that you must purchase the latest resources, adopt the newest management theories, and embrace current leadership mantras and trends. Like a slick salesman, it promises far more than it delivers and pockets a hefty profit along the way.

Sadly, the leadership industrial complex entangles too many aspiring leaders. Its books are in your stores. Its magazines are in your waiting rooms. Its strategies are in your churches. Its principles are in your homes. Its podcasts are on your smartphones. Its conferences are in your cities. Its products are in your social media feeds. Its talking points are in your ears. Its theories are in your workplaces. Its influence is on your families.

And, most likely, its thinking is in *your* head.

To repurpose an immortal line from Winston Churchill, never in human history has so much leadership material been made so widely available to so many but benefited so few.[1]

Is this not the case in our federal government? In Washington, D.C., we see an abundance of politicians but a dearth of leaders. Our society longs for courageous leaders who know when and where and how to take principled stands. Ironically, the proliferation of leadership materials has left a void of convictional, inspiring leaders.

This contrast is even more striking when we consider the great leaders of history. People like Martin Luther, George Washington, Abraham Lincoln, and Winston Churchill predated the modern leadership industrial complex, and they all led just fine without it.

The Ultimate Test Case

This book turns conventional leadership wisdom on its head. I am not a leadership expert hocking new insights or new approaches, nor do I plan to sell you a never-ending stream of leadership resources. In fact, I'll make another confession: if you're looking for a leadership guru, you're looking in the wrong place.

I believe faithful leadership is remarkably simple. Not easy, but simple. To be a faithful leader you likely need to do less, not more. Leadership, I'll argue, is largely intuitive, commonsensical, and, yes, spiritual in nature.

As evidence, I will give you an under-the-hood, behind-the-scenes look at the ultimate test case—an institution mired in crisis that has arisen over the past decade to become one of the largest and leading seminaries in the world. This fascinating story is proof positive that turnarounds can happen. We have experienced one. So can you.

This is more than a story of quantifiable gains. It's the story of an institutional renewal, an organizational transformation, and a comprehensive recovery that is not just intriguing but compelling. And this story is applicable to most every leader, actual or aspiring.

Whether you are an organizational executive, an institutional leader, a pastor serving a congregation, a volunteer in a nonprofit, a layperson engaging the marketplace, or a parent raising children, this book has something for you. This book will inspire and equip you to lead more fully and more competently.

I will remind you time and again that every leadership role boils down to one word: *stewardship*. Thus, not only can you lead faithfully, but you must.

Timeless Truths, Enduring Principles

The truths we'll explore are timeless, and the principles you will discover are enduring. I won't send you on a meandering, never-ending journey of leadership learning. That is the last thing you need.

Instead, I will remind you of the leadership principles that have always marked healthy organizations and those who preside over them, and then I'll show you how to lead accordingly.

Turnarounds don't happen accidentally. They happen when men and women embrace key principles and practices. These indispensable principles and practices—some learned from Scripture, others by common grace—ensure most anyone can lead and lead well.

And be encouraged, *anyone* includes you. You can up your leadership game, and I urge you to do so. As I said, ours is a treacherous age in which to lead. This is no time for the timid, the weak, or the ambivalent to hold the reins of power. On the contrary, we need our strongest leaders giving their best service toward ultimate, permanent ends. Our contextual crucible demands it.

And such a crucible is indeed a prism for leadership. Without the Roman Catholic Church's corruption, we would never have known Martin Luther's courage. Without the horrors of Nazism and the agony of the Battle of Britain, we would not have witnessed Winston Churchill's resolve. Without the world-jarring, overnight construction of the Berlin Wall, Ronald Reagan's words to Mikhail Gorbachev, "Tear down this wall," would not still ring in our ears.

Now is an exhilarating time to live and lead. You do not need Luther's or Churchill's life-or-death stage to prove your leadership mettle. You have your own crucible; embrace it. Own the stage God placed you on and recommit yourself to these first principles of leadership.

And that brings me to an important note. In addition to the ten principles we'll rediscover, keep your eye out for four longitudinal themes that run throughout this book. Each one could merit its own chapter, but they are more subtext than text, more supporting themes than essential principles.

While we are still setting the stage of the book, let's survey these longitudinal themes before going any further.

Longitudinal Theme 1: Lead Where You Are

The most important leadership role you will ever have is the one you're in right now. Or, to put it more succinctly, lead where you are.

By most any definition, I was a young man in a hurry. There is just something about being in your twenties that predestines restlessness. My mentor, Pastor Steve Lawson, sensed my restlessness and counseled me: "Jason, the most important job you will ever have is the one you have right now." His words registered on my heart before they landed in my ear. I still remember where we stood, by his administrative assistant's desk, when he spoke those words to me.

His instinct was right. I needed to hear his admonition. Not only did I need it, but in some ways I wanted it. I sensed that my unsettledness was unhealthy. I purposed that day, due to both the apparent spiritual principle and the obvious practical benefits, to live by those words. I encourage you to do the same.

As you read this book, know that I am not writing to your future self. I am writing to your current self. Leadership isn't just in your future. It's in your present. Scripture teaches that we are not guaranteed tomorrow, and even the most assured plans should come with a *deo volente*—if the Lord wills.

Along those lines, do not romanticize your future or daydream about how to seize it. Give your best energies to the position you currently hold. In leadership you are called to a stewardship of the present. And, in a very real sense, you will never have a greater stewardship than the one you have right now. We must work to maintain this mentality. Our self-help, self-improvement generation teaches us to strive for, to even connive for, our own betterment. But that is not the way of the faithful leader.

As an example, some have noted my father's generation viewed work like an escalator. You get on at a lower floor, remain faithful in your position and to your employer over the long haul, and, as the decades pass, you will ride the escalator up to higher floors.

My generation views employment more like a jungle gym, hopping from place to place, always scouring the horizon for self-advancement and never missing an opportunity for self-promotion. The leader's strategy for career advancement ought not resemble *American Ninja Warrior*.

Thus, to lead in the future, make sure you lead in the present. Do not spend your time refining your personal leadership philosophy; go with what you know now. Pursue faithfulness in leadership, not success. The world does not need more hypothetical leaders; it needs more actual ones.

In fact, Jesus commended such faithfulness, promising, "The one who is faithful in a very little thing is also faithful in much; and the one who is unrighteous in a very little thing is also unrighteous in much" (Luke 16:10). Vocationally, your today is more important than your tomorrow. The fastest way to a higher office is to excel in the one you occupy now.

Generally, those who serve most faithfully—who prove themselves indispensable to their organization's health—will not be overlooked. Such faithfulness is a rare trait, and employers work to retain such individuals. Indispensable employees usually do not have to fear pink slips and rarely must ask for pay raises.

I can assure you, if you faithfully lead where you are, it is unlikely you will be overlooked by man. And I can promise you, with the words of Christ in mind, you will not be overlooked by God.

This reassuring fact brings us to our next longitudinal theme: the providence of God.

Longitudinal Theme 2: God's Kind Providence

The second longitudinal theme that runs throughout this book is the kind providence of God, His sovereignty over all the cosmos put into action. It's been commonly described as the invisible hand of God in the glove of human circumstances. Think of it this way, when God's kind providence is working in your organization, 2+2 = 7. When he's not with you, 2 + 2 = 4, or even less.

God is not a slumbering deity past His prime and too fatigued to be of real assistance to you. Nor is He preoccupied, too engaged with the affairs of another world to give due attention to yours.

No, God is a micromanager. He cares about the affairs of this world, of my world, of your world. As you will see throughout these pages, time and time again God has worked in our institutional setting, and in my life personally, with remarkably kind providence. Indeed, He has lavished His kind providence upon us.

This is not false humility, nor is it contrived "Jesus talk." It is the absolute truth. And in this book, you will learn some unforgettable stories that make the point.

Yes, I want to be the kind of leader whom God delights in blessing. More broadly, we strive to be the kind of institution God finds easy to bless. In fact, we speak of this often at Midwestern Seminary. We seek to cultivate the right personal and institutional character, cling to the right mission, defend the right doctrines, and steward our resources all in a way that pleases the Lord—such that He will delight in blessing us.

Obviously, I write this book as a Bible-believing, evangelical Christian. For me, to speak of the providence of God is second nature, coming as naturally as talking about the weather. To see His mighty hand work and to sense His pleasure in our efforts bring inspiration and confidence. We believe He has led us thus far and will lead us further still.

Longitudinal Theme 3: Credibility Is Essential

Credibility is essential to leadership. If you show me a leader who lacks credibility, I will show you a leader who will soon lack followers. Show me an institution that lacks credibility, and I will show you an institution that will soon lack students and supporters. We intuitively know this to be true, but we must not overlook this aspect of leadership.

For example, consider a political candidate running for office. Nothing torpedoes a politician's campaign like an erosion of personal credibility. Flub a basic policy question, commit an unpardonable sin in your personal life, or appear uninspired about your own campaign, and donations will dry up, volunteers will lose interest, and paid staffers will even look for other opportunities. And, of course, voters, too, will turn their affections elsewhere.

Thus, credibility is essential, and it is a theme that runs throughout this book. When a leader enters the room, credibility had better enter with him. But credibility better not end with the leader; it must extend to his team and the entire enterprise he leads. And the sobering reality is that credibility takes years to accumulate but seconds to lose.

Longitudinal Theme 4: It Takes a Team

Faithful leadership takes a team. I devote an entire chapter to the team later, so I won't elaborate much here. But be on the lookout, in every chapter, for the team-oriented nature of leadership. You'll hear it loud and clear in some places and overhear it in others. But be listening for it everywhere.

As you read this book, you will sense the focus migrate from what marks the leader, to what marks the leadership team, to what marks the organization as a whole. This migration is intentional and natural. Transcendent leadership principles that shape healthy organizations are not merely preached from the top; they are embraced and embodied by the entire team.

Leadership is a top-down phenomenon, trickling down and around the organization. That especially includes the leadership team.

As to the Midwestern Seminary story, ultimately, all credit goes to God and His kind providence. Humanly speaking, credit goes far beyond me to the team God has given me. We have enjoyed remarkably long tenures together, have been blessed in our work, and have enjoyed more than our fair share of fun along the way.

As the old saying goes: "There's no I in team." There's also no "I" in the Midwestern Seminary story.

In Conclusion

As you read this book, I believe you will be inspired by a compelling institutional story, equipped through its leadership lessons, and relieved to know you will not have to reinvent yourself to lead faithfully. Most likely, you simply need to be emboldened to lead as you already know how.

That is my aim for you in writing this book. Make it your aim as you read it. And, as you will see, I am going to do my best to give you not just the *what* leaders should do, but also the *why* and the *how*.

So, with these ends in mind, let's move on to the first principle: know your context.

1

Know Your Context

When interpreting a text, there's a guiding principle every reader must keep in mind: context is king. You can't pluck a text out of its context and know the author's intended meaning for that text. You have to understand how it relates to the things around it.

For proper interpretation, the broader passage surrounding your text has as much to say about the meaning of the text as the text itself. Context is king, you see.

And the same is true in leadership: context trumps most everything else. Every leader is a leader in context. Every team is a team in context. Every organization is an organization in context. Every constituency served is a constituency in context. That's why you must know your context.

Recognizing your contextual realms—and recalibrating your leadership accordingly—is essential for the leader. The wise leader looks and learns, perceiving his contextual realms and appropriately adapting.

Now, lest you jump to unfounded conclusions, I'm not suggesting your core convictions or organizational mission are to be recalibrated. No, the permanent aspects of your life and leadership must hold steady, come what may. Convictional leaders have a compass, not an antenna. They stand with resolve on core truths, not on shifting sand.

But I am calling you to recognize the seasonal, changing aspects of your life and leadership. You see, significant aspects of your leadership are seasonal and must be revised based on these fluctuating variables. We'll review the most common ones in this chapter.

The first contextual realm we'll consider is the organizational context: Where does your organization find itself? What's its story? What are its strengths and weaknesses? Where is it in its life cycle? These are essential observations to make and necessary questions to answer.

And, as I'll argue throughout this book, you know this intuitively, don't you? One need not earn an advanced degree in leadership theory to sense the importance of your context. You simply need to be reminded of this and nudged to think in these terms.

To set the stage, consider the institutional context of Midwestern Seminary in 2012.

Midwestern Seminary: An Institution in Context

Every leader *inherits* a context.

The leader's inherited context is like sitting down to a never-ending game of chess. All of your predecessors played this continual game over the course of many years. As I surveyed this metaphorical chessboard, some pieces were already off the board, while other pieces were in unintended, unhelpful locations.

But this is Leadership 101, is it not? Leadership is necessary because people and organizations are often suboptimal. Therefore, to lead is to sit down in the leadership chair, slide it up to the table, survey the chessboard as it is—not as you wish it were—and resume the game.

As I write this book, Midwestern Baptist Theological Seminary stands as one of the largest and leading seminaries in the world. By most every traditional marker of a seminary's health, Midwestern Seminary ranks at or near the top. But that hasn't always been the case. In fact, it once was far from it. To understand the story, we must go back, way back—not just to 2012, but to the mid-twentieth century.

Founded in Controversy, Mired in Controversy

Southern Baptists founded Midwestern Seminary in 1957. Like most every other corner of Protestantism, the postwar era brought dramatic growth to the Southern Baptist Convention. Reading the history of the annual denominational meetings is to be teleported back to another time and place. It seems like an altogether foreign land.

Collectively, denominational optimism and ambition were at flood tide. Perhaps this spirit is most evidenced in the 1954 denominational theme, "A Million More in '54." That slogan championed the SBC's effort to add one million new church members in the year 1954.

Dramatic numerical growth—and the accompanying financial resources—made denominational expansion not just desired, but possible. Thus, in those years the SBC expanded its institutional footprint. Midwestern Seminary became—and remains—the SBC's newest seminary, founded in 1957.[1]

But the founding was not without controversy. As the adage goes, where you find two Baptists, you'll find at least three opinions. After moving past the first debated point of whether to launch a sixth seminary, the next, more controversial question was where to locate it.

As the SBC considered locations for its new seminary, St. Louis, Kansas City, Denver, Chicago, Jacksonville, and Memphis emerged as finalists. Ultimately, Kansas City was best positioned to satisfy the three main criteria: (1) Be close enough to the denomination's base to draw students. (2) Be located north and west enough to serve underserved areas. (3) Be positioned to alleviate the enrollment burdens on the existing SBC seminaries, especially the ones located in Louisville and Fort Worth.

Thus, in 1957 Midwestern Seminary launched with the anticipated fanfare. In the ensuing months, the board of trustees quickly selected the seminary's first president, Dr. Millard Berquist, secured a temporary meeting space, assembled a faculty, purchased acreage for a new campus, began construction on the first cluster of institutional buildings, and recruited an incoming class of students, even as they tidied up all the other myriad of issues associated with birthing an institution.

The Elliott Controversy

The upstart institution began with much promise, but the new paint was barely dry when conflict erupted. The controversy shook not just the campus, but the entire denomination and the religious landscape far beyond.

Known as the "Elliott Controversy," the conflict centered on faculty member Ralph Elliott's new book, *The Message of Genesis*. The book, which questioned essential doctrines like biblical inspiration and inerrancy, landed as a bombshell on the denominational landscape.

The struggle lasted more than two years, culminating in Elliott's termination for insubordination. Beyond Elliott, the controversy metastasized into broader concerns (which history would prove to be justified) about the doctrinal integrity of the faculty.

The Elliott Controversy triggered a revision to the denomination's confessional statement, *The Baptist Faith and Message*, in 1963, and it foreshadowed the broader Battle for the Bible that would engulf the denomination in the 1980s.

The Elliott Controversy lingered long after its namesake departed. Even now, some sixty years later, I occasionally get asked if Ralph Elliott still teaches at Midwestern Seminary. The leadership lessons to learn from the Elliott Controversy are innumerable.

The Battle for the Bible

As the seminary sought to move past the Elliott Controversy, the broader Battle for the Bible heated up. Rumblings occurred throughout the 1960s and '70s, with periodic confrontations and denominational skirmishes. Clearly, dissonance between the denomination's leaders (who ostensibly served SBC churches) and the people in the pews was intensifying.

These tensions erupted in 1979 and played out with unimaginable intensity over the next thirteen years. Known as the Conservative Resurgence, it was a denomination-wide, winner-take-all death match.

On one side was the denomination's left-leaning entities and those who supported them, whether due to doctrinal appreciation, fear of a "fundamentalist takeover," a distaste for the political tactics of movement conservatives, or as a simple desire to preserve the status quo.

On the other side were those committed to the conservative agenda. They affirmed key doctrines like the inspiration and inerrancy of Scripture, and they strategized to wrest control of the convention by winning sequential presidential elections.

The conservatives promised to use the convention president's appointive powers to populate the entities with conservative trustees. Over time, the trustees would replace the entity executives, clarify and enforce existing doctrinal statements, and appoint new, conservative faculty members.

Leadership Turnover

Midwestern Seminary was positioned near the bull's-eye of denominational concern. And its position in the crosshairs was altogether justified.

Its faculty was clearly to the left of the churches they were paid to serve. Thus, as the conservative plan unfolded and conservative trustees gained a majority on the board, the seminary's retirement-aged chief executive, Dr. Milton Ferguson, vacated the president's office.

Dr. Ferguson's retirement in 1995 paved the way for Midwestern Seminary to elect its third president, Dr. Mark Coppenger. Coppenger was a recognized scholar and a committed conservative. His military background undergirded a no-nonsense leadership style, which fortified him as he reshaped the faculty to better align with the SBC's theological conservativism.

However, Coppenger's directness at times proved to be a bit much, thus putting him at odds with the seminary's board of trustees and leading to his departure in 1999.

As the new century dawned, Midwestern elected its fourth president, Dr. Phil Roberts, in early 2001. Serving for eleven years, Dr. Roberts led the institution through several ambitious initiatives. He added and sold campus acreage, launched new academic programs, and, most ambitiously, undertook a major building campaign.

Roberts's leadership style led to staff turnover and, like Coppenger, conflict with the board of trustees. This tension resulted in Roberts's eventual departure in February 2012.

A Trend Has Developed

By now, you've detected a trend, and it's not a good one; theological controversy, institutional conflict, financial scarcity, and forced leadership changes were constants throughout the seminary's history. So much so, these ever-present concerns prompted the denomination to contemplate closing Midwestern Seminary in the mid 2000s.

To many, Midwestern Seminary looked like a fifty-year-long fire that needed to be extinguished. And it didn't take a critical eye to come to that conclusion. Those were the facts.

Thankfully, Southern Baptists proved resilient again by staying the course with Midwestern Seminary and keeping her alive to fight another day.

Midwestern Seminary, 2012

As I surveyed the institution in 2012, controversy was still apparent. From a distance, I knew Midwestern Seminary was in need, but looking back, it was far weaker than I perceived.

Campus Facilities

To the eye, the campus facilities were in an obvious state of disrepair. Most of the buildings were original to their mid-twentieth-century construction, the only difference being the additional decades of wear and tear. The interior of these buildings looked like abandoned bureaucratic office space from a failed Soviet state.

In fact, a friend warned me, "Jason, Midwestern Seminary has the prettiest grounds but the ugliest buildings in the SBC." Another denominational leader bluntly told me, "Jason, every building on the campus needs to be razed. You need to bulldoze every building or comprehensively renovate each one. You'll have no other options."

Most alarmingly, a well-respected, former professor of mine warned me that to go to Kansas City was to jeopardize my future ministry. The seminary was altogether irrecoverable, he soberly warned me.

In fact, the campus was so unappealing that the trustees didn't even meet at the seminary but, rather, at a nearby hotel. What is more, my presidential interviews took place in remote cities. Thus, by the time I accepted their nomination, I'd never even seen the campus. Given the dilapidated buildings, I can't help but think that was intentional. Reflecting on that fact makes me smile to this day.

At the time of this book's publishing, we've been able to renovate nearly every building on campus and have added a new, 42,000-square-foot student center. Instead of being a liability, our campus facilities are now first-class; they're a true institutional asset and a source of denominational pride. All told, over the past decade we've allocated some $45,000,000 to these projects, without incurring any long-term debt along the way.

Enrollment

On the enrollment front, Midwestern Seminary had just over a thousand students enrolled in the 2010–2011 academic year. The average accredited seminary in North America has a total enrollment of about three hundred students, so the enrollment was relatively strong.[2] Supportive churches and entrepreneurial administrators made this possible.

But even so, we've enjoyed dramatic gains over the past decade. We now enjoy a total enrollment of approximately five thousand students, and this is in a higher-education context (there's that word again) where most institutions are plateaued or declining. In fact, over the past decade we've consistently been recognized as the fastest—or among the fastest—growing theological institutions in North America.

Contextual awareness recognizes how unparalleled this growth has been, but it also recognizes that, ultimately, no institution is immune to outgoing tides and stiff headwinds. This is to say, we would lack gratitude not to celebrate our enrollment growth, but we'd lack wisdom to plan and spend like it will continue into the future.

Finances

On the financial front, the situation was bleaker still. We were barren, a financial wasteland. The previous year's academic budget was close to $9,000,000, but our revenues were closer to $8,000,000. Complicating matters even more, the previous administration had launched an ambitious construction project—a new chapel complex—but due to a lack of funds, it had been stalled out for over a year.

When I arrived on campus, I understood the financial difficulties to be in the past, but I quickly learned that they were very much in the present. I vividly recall unpacking my office as the interim CFO informed me that we might not meet payroll. I was alarmed but helpless. What could be done at this late hour?

Further complicating matters, the seminary had functioned under formal financial austerity the past several years. In fact, on two separate occasions employees' salaries were involuntarily reduced and benefits were cut. On multiple occasions, key churches and donors had bailed out the seminary, enabling them to meet payroll at the eleventh hour.

When I arrived, Midwestern desperately needed good news. So much so, the last thing I could afford to do (no pun intended) was declare financial exigency. Everyone knew the seminary was financially frail, but we desperately needed to move forward. An institution can't move forward by making U-turns. We could not be drawn back into public financial hardship and all the accompanying questions and accusations about what got us there.

We'll explore this more later in the book, but we managed to slog our way through the opening years of financial hardship and have long since moved beyond those difficulties. At the time of this book's publishing, our annual revenues exceed $30,000,000, up from $8,000,000 in 2010–2011. The seminary's total net assets are north of $80,000,000, up from just over $20,000,000 a decade ago.

Academics

As to academic credibility, we had work to do on that front too. I inherited a devoted faculty, but they were largely undistinguished. Due to insufficient resources, a lack of seminary emphasis on scholarly output, and the more urgent concern of personal and institutional survival, who could fault them?

Then, our academic output, as tallied by books published, articles written, and scholarly presentations delivered, was almost undetectable. We hardly registered in those categories, and, for an institution of higher learning, those categories matter.

Since then, we've resourced our existing faculty to flourish, added top-notch scholars to their number, and prioritized institutional achievement in these areas. In the world of evangelical seminaries, our faculty now ranks second to none. Annually, we are at or near the top in scholarly output with our faculty members garnering the high praise they deserve.

Campus Morale

Lastly, we should briefly consider campus morale. As you can imagine, the depressing circumstances created a toxic brew. Many of our best employees had fled to other opportunities. Many of the remaining employees were plotting to do the same. Still others chose to keep their heads down, just trying to survive. The seminary was a beleaguered institution, and those who served it tended to be as well.

Such was our organizational context in 2012. Morale and resources were scarce. Liabilities and controversies were abundant. The prospects seemed bleak, with conflict and failure a recurring reality throughout the institution's history, including its recent history. And, to be candid, I didn't know the half of it on day one. I knew the past difficulties, but I didn't know the present ones, nor did many of the trustees or remaining employees.

Know Your Personal Context

What about you?

What's your organizational context? What's its history? What besetting challenges has it faced? What are your resources and liabilities? Your challenges and opportunities? How have your predecessors fared in your position? As Peter Drucker argued, if people consistently fail in the position, the problem is likely with the position, not the people.[3]

For you, contextual awareness begins with your organization, but it doesn't end there. It must get personal—and fast.

Self-knowledge is a difficult pursuit, but it is a necessary one for the leader. John Calvin began his *Institutes of the Christian Religion* (one of the greatest systematic theologies of all time) by arguing, "Nearly all wisdom we possess, that is to say, true and sound wisdom, consists of two parts: the knowledge of God and of ourselves."[4] Calvin was right. You, the leader, must prioritize self-knowledge.

I'm not given to navel-gazing, so self-knowledge is difficult. I'm generally skeptical of personality tests and similar instruments that type us. But during the presidential interview process, I stumbled into a self-discovery that was as accurate as it was revealing.

Presidential interview processes tend to be much longer and more grueling than you might imagine. For me, that was certainly the case. From start to finish, it played out over nearly six months. It was one-half year of excruciating suspense, constant prayer, and exhausting uncertainty.

When the presidential search committee informed me that I was their choice, they quickly added that it was contingent on four final tests, in addition to a collection of reference contacts. The final four criteria were no less serious than the previous rounds of questions, but, chronologically, it made the most sense to position them at the end.

Four Final Tests

The first test was satisfactorily passing a criminal background check. I shrugged at that request, knowing I'd be as clean as a whistle. Next they mentioned a personal financial audit. Again, I had no concern on that front. We'd been in ministry for fifteen years and hadn't made a lot of money, but we'd avoided debt and had been wise stewards along the way.

Third, they ordered up for me a thorough, executive physical. At the age of thirty-five and as a former athlete, that request didn't spark any concern, but it did puzzle me. I didn't see it coming, but they assured me it was common to executive searches. After all, no organization wants to hire a leader only to discover he's not physically up to the task.

The last request concerned me. The presidential search committee mandated I undergo an executive psychological evaluation. Like the physical, I didn't anticipate the request, but unlike the physical, I had difficulty envisioning why it was requested or how it would go.

I had never undergone a psychological evaluation. In fact, other than a few premarital counseling sessions my wife and I enjoyed, I'd always been on the other side of such meetings.

But here I was, slated for a day's worth of psychological exams. To be forthright, I dreaded the day. It felt like a lose-lose proposition. I recall joking with my wife, in advance, with a sort of gallows humor.

I envisioned myself reclining on a couch and being probed with questions, Bob Newhart style. "Did your father spank you as a child?" If I answered no, they'd probably conclude I was self-centered and self-entitled. If I answered yes, they'd conclude I was prone to volatile, abusive behavior. I felt as though I was predestined for a day of drudgery, only to be punished by the findings.

Frankly, it may have been the most exhausting day of my life, and it was altogether different from what I envisioned. Yes, there were some questions about my childhood, but the day was spent mainly on exercises to test powers of recollection, cognition, and reasoning.

At the end of the day, the evaluator issued a full report, most all of which was interesting. But the most illuminating part was his observation: "Dr. Allen, you were reared in what we call an 'achievement household,' thus you're an achiever by nature, and you're motivated to pursue goals and accomplishments."

My goodness, I thought, *he's spot-on.* As I joke, in the Allen family we had Junior Achievement—junior better get out and achieve something. The two primary areas of achievement were academic and athletic, but the givenness to achieve permeated most every area of life, from our daily chores to recreational fishing.

I left that day's evaluation feeling like my examiner had put his finger on exactly who I was; what, under God, made me that way; and how that mentality would show up in my institutional leadership.

I'd come to find that session helpful, not just to better know myself but to know the importance of a leader being emotionally equipped for executive office. After all, leadership isn't just an IQ test. We all know highly intelligent people who aren't cut out for leadership. Yes, you must be sufficiently knowledgeable in your specific field, but you don't have to be brilliant, in the formal definition, to lead.

In his book *View from the Top*, Michael Lindsay dials in on the significance of emotional intelligence. Ponder his words carefully:

> Emotional intelligence, popularized by Daniel Goleman in 1995, is "the capacity for recognizing our own feelings and those of others, for motivating ourselves, and for managing emotions well

in ourselves and in our relationships." Goleman's work adapts the work of earlier psychologists and includes five competencies: awareness of one's own emotions, regulating one's own emotions, being able to motivate oneself, sensing the feelings of others, and handling emotions in relationships well.

In his book, *Working with Emotional Intelligence*, Goleman claims that "IQ takes second position to emotional intelligence in job performance." In a comparison of competence models for 181 organizations, Goleman concluded that 67 percent of the abilities deemed essential for effective performance were emotional capacities.

Based on a similar analysis of competencies for U.S.-government jobs and research he commissioned on executive leadership positions, Goleman observed that "the higher the level of the job, the less important technical skills and cognitive abilities were and the more important competence in emotional intelligence became."[5]

As I said, I'm generally skeptical of personality tests, believing they tend to overly type people, and they can often lead to a "that's just the way I am" mentality. But you should strive to know yourself. For instance, organizational theorist Peter Drucker famously argued that leaders must know whether they work best in the mornings or at night and whether they process information best audibly or visually.[6]

So, how about you? What has made you who you are? What motivates you; what discourages you? What incentivizes you; what disincentivizes you? Are you task oriented, or are you relationally oriented? Do you find goals energizing or intimidating? Are you sanguine by nature or prone to cloudiness?

While I am not suggesting you must undergo a psychological evaluation, I am suggesting that to effectively lead, you must know who you are and you must know your personal context.

Don't Forget Your Family

If you are married, your personal context includes your spouse and the children God has given you to raise. These glorious commitments are not incidental to your life and leadership; they are essential. And you should treat them as such.

First, you'll need to keep your ambition in check so as not to wreck the family God has given you. Too many travel as though their goal in life is to accumulate frequent-flyer awards. Or they hop from job to job seeking to climb a career ladder, but they end up leaving their family behind as they do.

There are life stages, especially when your children are young, when surviving is success. For example, consider our move to Kansas City to serve Midwestern Seminary. At that time, our children were ages nine to four. Four years earlier, moving our five children may have proven too much. Four years later, the kids' friendships and emotional ties to Louisville, Kentucky (our then home), would've made relocation exceedingly painful for them.

Likewise, their life stages matter. As I write this book, we have five (*five!*) teenagers. These years have proven to be sweet ones too, but they require different levels of engagement. A decade ago, I put my children to bed at 8:00 p.m. and would work late into the night. Now, I wake early, knowing my evenings will be given to them.

Lastly, know your family's giftings, interests, and comfort zones. If your spouse is shy, don't nudge her into public speaking. If she's disorganized, don't insist she coordinate a program.

Ask yourself: *What's my family's stage? What does my spouse need of me? What do our children need from us? Are they flourishing? Is it likely they'll flourish in a potential place of service?*

Know Your Team Members

As you've already detected and as we'll explore more thoroughly later, your organization will not rise beyond the team who serves it. Knowing this as a leader, you must steward your team with care.

As a seminary president, my primary responsibility is to recruit and retain the right people to help us recruit and retain students, friends, and supporters. Thus, I work to know my team. So should you. We'll explore the team more in chapter 6, but, for now, let's consider just one aspect of your team—their context or, we might say, their life stage.

Many leaders stop learning about their team members when they hire them. For the wise leader, that's just the beginning of the relationship, not the apex. For instance, you should observe the life stage of your team members and attempt to lead them through these stages accordingly. I call this the Cool Hand Luke factor.

The Cool Hand Luke Factor

You might remember the classic film. When I was a kid, it aired on TBS monthly it seemed, and I watched it more times than I can count. You likely recall the story line. Paul Newman starred as Luke (dubbed Cool Hand Luke by his prison mates). In a night of drunkenness, he foolishly sawed the tops off parking meters.

Luke's offense was a relatively minor one. All he had to do was serve his brief sentence and he'd be out of prison in short order. But in the mid-twentieth century, Luke and his fellow inmates were treated as slave labor. And to ensure order, the warden (known as "Boss"), ruled with an iron fist.

The inmates worked on chain gangs, laboring in the sweltering heat and humidity of the Deep South. Luke was a freethinker and couldn't abide the confines of prison or the heavy-handedness of his overseers.

Thus, he escaped three times, being caught the first two and—spoiler alert!—killed on his final run.

To punish those who fled and to dissuade others from even considering it, Boss tortured Luke. Guards subjected Luke to merciless beatings, around-the-clock ditchdigging, and protracted confinements in "the Box."

One scene serves as an object lesson for this chapter. While in prison, Luke received word that his mother had died. The warden preemptively locked Luke in the Box. The warden then reflected that when prisoners learn of their mother's death they tend to get "rabbit in their blood," running to attend their mother's funeral.

Life Stages That Matter to Them Should Matter to You

You see the point, don't you? The wise leader observes team members' life stages. The leader doesn't coerce them to stay, but he does shepherd them, with additional care, through such seasons. And certain life stages are particularly unsettling. Degree completion, the death of a parent, turning forty, and the empty-nest stage are all times of natural disruption, reflection, and potential transition.

Closer to home, many of my team members are roughly my age. Helping them navigate, at the personal level, major life transition points is a way I can serve them well. The point isn't that employees can't leave. I lead an institution, not a prison camp. Our employees aren't conscripted. They're here by choice. But I want them to leave due to a clear sense of calling elsewhere and the accompanying certainty and joy that come with it. Not due to my personal or institutional oversight.

So, ask yourself: *How is my relationship with my team members? Am I investing most in those who invest most in my organization? Am I observant and aware of their life stages? Do I strategically serve them in moments of grief or seasons of turmoil? Do I set before them a map for their future, helping them chart their course in my organization?*

Know Your Constituency

Finally, you must know the constituency your organization serves. And I don't mean that in the abstract. Work to sense the contextual moment and, thus, contextual needs, of those you serve. At Midwestern Seminary, we have two primary constituencies: the students we train, and then, through our graduates, the churches they serve.

Our churches are in a needy state. Most congregations in America, regardless of the denomination, are plateaued or declining. As America continues to secularize, these challenges will likely intensify. Thus, our churches need ministers who are convictional, impassioned, and well equipped for service.

Similarly, our students face challenges unlike previous generations. Affordability and accessibility are always on their minds, and they should be on my mind and the minds of others on my leadership team.

So it is for you. *Whom do you serve? What are their needs? Which challenges are unique to your constituency? Which challenges are long-standing? Which ones are new and intensifying?*

In Conclusion

In the same way a reader works to rightly understand the context of a passage, you must work to know your contextual moment. In most every component of your leadership, context will impact how you lead, and that context is evolving. So must you.

Continue to ask yourself key questions. *What does your organization most need? What does your constituency most expect? What does your team most desire? What does your family most require of you? What can you, uniquely, contribute?*

And you sense the importance of context intuitively, right? You can't know which way to go until you know where you are.

Leadership doesn't occur in a vacuum. It occurs in context. And that context is king. Principle 1: Know your context.

2

Hold Your Convictions

In geopolitics, ambiguity usually leads to disaster. For proof positive, one need look no further than the Korean Peninsula. In the early 1950s, the United States' failure to communicate its intent to defend South Korea led to the Korean War, a war that's officially never ended.

Sometimes such ambiguity is accidental. Believe it or not, other times, it's intentional. In fact, "strategic ambiguity" is a carefully developed foreign-policy position. Some nations choose strategic ambiguity. They deem it best not to make clear their intended response to a potential scenario.

For example, strategic ambiguity has long been the United States' official defense posture toward Taiwan, an ambiguity that's led to heightened tensions in the South China Sea.

Taiwan, as you may recall, is an island democracy located approximately one hundred miles from mainland China. When China fell to Communism in 1949, its government fled to Taiwan, as have other freedom-seeking Chinese. Since then, Taiwan has developed into a functioning democracy with a vibrant economy.

However, Communist China views Taiwan as a breakaway province—one that must be brought back under Beijing's control, by force, if necessary. And the People's Liberation Army has expanded rapidly the past two decades with that end in mind. Thus, the recent spike in tensions, the constant saber-rattling from Beijing, and the prevailing question: What will the United States do if China moves across the Taiwan Strait on their "renegade province"?

As you can tell, these are weighty matters with grave consequences. I question the value of strategic ambiguity in foreign affairs. I altogether reject it when it comes to an organization's convictions.

Sadly, many organizations operate with *convictional ambiguity*, an ambiguity that's not accidental. It's intentional, strategic on their part. Such entities, and those who lead them, choose strategic ambiguity for political or pragmatic reasons. They deem the costs associated with taking clear stands to be too high. Expediency wins the day.

Closer to Home, the Mushy Middle

I encountered what I would later identify as "institutional strategic ambiguity" my first year on the job. Shortly after my election as Midwestern Seminary president, I found myself conversing with a seminary president from another denomination. Trying to be a good neighbor and to better know the lay of the land in my region, I initiated the visit.

I knew both the doctrinal orientation of her faculty and the leanings of the churches of her denomination. Thus, I sensed the institution was very much out of line with the church members they ostensibly served. On theological issues like the inspiration and inerrancy of the Bible and the exclusivity of the gospel, there was a wide berth. On the great cultural flash points, like issues related to human sexuality, gender, marriage, the right to life, etc., that institution was also far to the left of its churches.

But as I entered her office that day, I was reminded anew of how distant our two institutions were, even though we both have Baptist in our name.

As we talked, she confirmed that, indeed, her institution was to the left of her denomination's churches. I was not accusatory, nor was she evasive. We just candidly discussed theological education in North America and where our institutions fit into that landscape.

The more we talked, the more my curiosity was piqued. Finally, it got the best of me. I just couldn't help myself. I framed her situation just as I did for you in the previous paragraphs; then I asked her how she managed the apparent tension between her institution and the churches of her denomination.

She concurred with my analysis, acknowledging the dynamics existed much as I described. I was still curious how she managed this tension, so I inquired further: "Considering these two realities, what's your plan?"

With candor, she admitted their strategy was "to hang out in the mushy middle as long as possible." Her response didn't really surprise me. It is the standard play for institutions in her predicament.

You see, the seminaries of many denominations are far more progressive than the churches they ostensibly serve. In a twist of irony, this scenario leads to these institutions undermining the churches they were founded to strengthen.

Strategic ambiguity in such institutional settings is deeply problematic for two reasons. First, it has failed morally in principle. Second, it will fail in practice pragmatically. Let's think more deeply on this scenario.

Flawed in Principle, Unsustainable in Practice

There are many ways to categorize seminaries: large or small, endowed or unendowed, accredited or unaccredited, Protestant or Roman Catholic. But the most important distinction is confessional or nonconfessional.

A confessional institution is clear about what it believes and teaches. By covenant and contract, professors believe and teach in accordance with and not contrary to the institution's statement(s) of faith.

The confessional statement is more than a historic document, buried in past trustee minutes. Rather, it lives at the institution's front and center. The faculty and staff know that it's regulatory, as do watching constituencies.

Nonconfessional institutions have rejected doctrinal commitments altogether or, more commonly, have just chosen to ignore them. They often have a formal statement of faith, but everyone knows it means little. It's a reference point to a bygone era. It doesn't represent the seminary's current beliefs, much less protect those beliefs for future generations.

Nonconfessional institutions often exist in strategic ambiguity, but they do so immorally. They're violating their formal doctrinal commitments, and they're undermining the churches and constituencies they've been charged to serve.

What is more, they've acted treacherously against past generations of supporters and stakeholders. Altogether, it's a slimy and immoral practice. From start to finish, it's flawed in principle.

But it's also unsustainable in practice. The mushy middle is quickly giving way. Ideological polarization is setting in. Secularism is on the march. Increasingly, onlookers demand to know what you affirm and what you disavow. They expect to know what you believe, endorse, tolerate, and reject.

These expectations aren't just for theological institutions. They're for most every organization with a constituency. Businesses hear from their customers, nonprofits from their supporters, suppliers from their vendors, and entities from their stakeholders.

To be clear, I'm not suggesting you must have a public opinion on every issue of the day. Midwestern Seminary doesn't take a position on issues that aren't germane to our convictions or our mission. Our institutional indifference to these matters isn't so much strategic as it is natural.

I may have opinions on marginal tax rates, the nuances of national immigration policy, or whether we should intervene militarily in the South China Sea, but they're not relevant to the vision, mission, or convictions of Midwestern Seminary.

On issues that intersect with our mission and our confessional commitments, we speak, and we speak confidently.

Let's further tease out organizational conviction by taking a closer look at theological education and, more specifically, Midwestern Seminary. I realize you most likely don't lead a theological institution, but, again, the institution I lead serves as our case study. But before getting to Midwestern Seminary, I must go back, way back to the mid-nineteenth century.

Convictional Clarity and Organizational Accountability

Southern Baptist churches founded their first seminary in 1859. Though Southern Baptist seminaries are now much in line with the denomination's confessional statement—the *Baptist Faith and Message 2000*—such has not always been the case. Indeed, the history of theological education indicates the need for churches to keep an ever-vigilant eye on the seminaries they own.

Moreover, the New Testament instructs the church to cherish, defend, and proclaim the truth. Paul designates the church "the pillar and support of the truth" (1 Tim. 3:15). The faithful seminary co-labors with the churches it serves to this end.

Rightly related, the seminary and the church enjoy a symbiotic relationship. The churches hold the seminaries theologically accountable and send them students to train. The seminaries graduate those students to serve the churches as pastors and ministers who are reinforced biblically and doctrinally. A mutually beneficial cycle of theological faithfulness should exist, but, again, that's often not the case.

More than Signatures

No single act more clearly communicates an institution's commitment to confessional fidelity than when a professor publicly signs the seminary's statement of faith. The signing is a communal reminder of the institution's doctrinal commitment, but the act alone is insufficient.

Many seminaries' confessional statements are littered with signatures that proved not to have been rendered in good faith. In fact, many of the names are now infamous in Southern Baptist life, such as C. H. Toy and Dale Moody, to name a few. Ironically, the first signer of Midwestern Seminary's Articles of Faith was Ralph Elliott, whose story we touched on in the previous chapter.

Maintaining Vigilance

We must recognize that, at the very least, the embers of the world burn within us all. Indwelling sin, the allure of the academy, and the riptide-like pull of an increasingly secular culture all necessitate alertness and diligence.

Moreover, seminaries must not treat churches paternalistically, thinking they know the churches' needs better than the churches themselves. The seminary's role is not to prod, drag, or enlighten the churches theologically. The seminary does not sit in judgment of the church; the church sits in judgment of the seminary.

Confessional faithfulness demands that we remain vigilant. We must seek to anticipate doctrinal drift, to perceive where theological slippage may occur. Theological faithfulness must also include a relentless refusal to settle for obliqueness; probing and distilling questions are never out of bounds. This is key. Ambiguity is the incubator of doctrinal infidelity.

At a seminary, the instrument for doctrinal accountability is a confessional statement, but it is only as meaningful as the integrity of the one signing it and only as helpful as the courage and care of those charged with enforcing it. This oversight begins with the seminary's administration, but it includes the board of trustees, and it encompasses the churches that own the seminary.

Your Convictions Are Essential to Your Mission

As the Constitutional Convention adjourned in Philadelphia in 1787, a woman approached Benjamin Franklin and asked: "Mr. Franklin, what kind of government have you given us?" "A republic, madam," Franklin replied, "if you can keep it."

Such is the case for many theological institutions. They've received an inheritance of faithfulness. The current leaders must steward that, faithful to the organization's convictions, for the next generation. And, as you do, know that it's essential for mission faithfulness. The convictions undergird and protect the mission. The mission is powered forward by the convictions.

Having reviewed theological education and Midwestern Seminary, let's now think more holistically about conviction, especially organizational conviction.

Defining and Describing Conviction

Conviction is a confidence, rooted in principled clarity and moral certainty, of the rightness of your position and that your stand isn't just appropriate but essential. Put another way, conviction isn't just the assurance that you're right, but that being right matters. And it's to demonstrate, when it matters most, the courage of those convictions.

Conviction, too, is contextual. It's easy to be resolved in the abstract, but conviction only truly matters in contexts of adversity, with real or potential hardship. As Thomas Carlyle famously put it: "But indeed, Conviction, were it never so excellent, is worthless till it convert itself into Conduct.[1]

My friend Albert Mohler helpfully writes: "A conviction is a belief of which we are thoroughly convinced. I don't mean that we are merely persuaded that something is true, but rather that we are convinced this truth is essential and life-changing. We live out this truth and are willing to die for it."[2]

To better grasp conviction, consider with me two illuminating passages of Scripture. The first, from the Old Testament, is well known by Jews, Christians, and non-Christians alike. The second, from the New Testament, is more obscure. Both passages tell the story of individuals who demonstrated the courage of their convictions in the face of life-or-death consequences.

The Old Testament passage is a tale of monarchial overreach, idolatry resisted, persecution endured, and preservation through flames of fire. Simply put, it's a tale of unyielding conviction. And note, these are ordinary people, but they demonstrate extraordinary courage.

> Nebuchadnezzar answered and said to them, "Is it true, O Shadrach, Meshach, and Abednego, that you do not serve my gods or worship the golden image that I have set up? Now if you are ready when you hear the sound of the horn, pipe, lyre, trigon, harp, bagpipe, and every kind of music, to fall down and worship the image that I have made, well and good. But if you do not worship, you shall immediately be cast into a burning fiery furnace. And who is the god who will deliver you out of my hands?"

Shadrach, Meshach, and Abednego answered and said to the king, "O Nebuchadnezzar, we have no need to answer you in this matter. If this be so, our God whom we serve is able to deliver us from the burning fiery furnace, and he will deliver us out of your hand, O king. But if not, be it known to you, O king, that we will not serve your gods or worship the golden image that you have set up." (Dan. 3:14–18 ESV)

Notice the resolve of these faithful, young Jews before the most powerful man in the world. They held their convictions—faithfulness to the one true God—boldly.

In response, God did the miraculous. He spared them so that "the fire had not had any power over [their] bodies . . . The hair of their heads was not singed, their cloaks were not harmed, and no smell of fire had come upon them" (3:27). As a result, Nebuchadnezzar was amazed, praised God, and gave Shadrach, Meshach, and Abednego promotions in the kingdom of Babylon (3:28–30).

However, I must acknowledge that having this type of conviction does not always have a happy ending. Church history is filled with names of those who died as martyrs. The point is not assured deliverance. The point is faithfulness in the face of scorn, ostracism, and even persecution.

Indeed, this type of conviction can be costly, but if one is willing to compromise in difficult circumstances, then maybe they never really had true conviction to begin with. Perhaps they held opinions rather than convictions. You see, opinions change when push comes to shove. Conviction is rooted and grounded and is not subject to the whim of circumstances.

Next, the New Testament relates a tale of similar courage and similar consequences. Here, shortly after Jesus's death and resurrection, the apostles Peter and John preached in the face of fierce opposition—but not just opposition, actual persecution:

Now when they saw the boldness of Peter and John, and perceived that they were uneducated, common men, they were astonished. And they recognized that they had been with Jesus. But seeing the man who was healed standing beside them, they had nothing to say in opposition. But when they had commanded them to leave the council, they conferred with one another, saying, "What shall we do with these men? For that a notable sign has been performed through them is evident to all the inhabitants of Jerusalem, and we cannot deny it. But in order that it may spread no further among the people, let us warn them to speak no more to anyone in this name." So they called them and charged them not to speak or teach at all in the name of Jesus. But Peter and John answered them, "Whether it is right in the sight of God to listen to you rather than to God, you must judge, for we cannot but speak of what we have seen and heard." And when they had further threatened them, they let them go, finding no way to punish them, because of the people, for all were praising God for what had happened. (Acts 4:13–21 ESV)

Do you see the convictional courage on display in this passage? Regardless of the cost, Peter and John were resolute; they could not help but preach about Jesus and what He had done. They did not just hold their convictions; they spoke them boldly.

For both biblical stories, we must note that these men weren't needlessly offensive. They weren't pugnacious by nature. Pointless provocation was not their forte. No, they were far from that.

That's why we mustn't confuse antagonism with conviction. Some men are like children at recess, picking fights with others just for the sport of it. This isn't conviction, but immaturity and paranoia. Conviction often looks like steel covered by velvet. Firmness delivered with kindness. Fortitude baptized in compassion.

We mustn't assume in our day that the proper venue for convictional stands is social media. In fact, social media is often the worst medium. Hand-to-hand combat on Twitter is usually unproductive. Such harsh, shrill, pointless debate is not what we find in Scripture, and it's certainly not what we see in the previous passages. It most likely will not help your organization.

Faithful, biblical conviction is the courage to speak when others demand silence. It's the strength to stand when others bow. It's the commitment to obey God rather than man. That's the type of convictional leadership our generation—and your organization—desperately need.

Conviction, Operationally Important

Organizational conviction begins with leaders. No one has ever been inspired by a fainting flower. But while conviction must start with the leader, it must get beyond him to the team. Conviction must pulsate from the leader until it permeates the entire entity.

This is true in matters of ideology, doctrinal or otherwise. But it's also true operationally in how your organization functions. Operational conviction means you're willing to turn conventional wisdom on its head. Industry-standard practices shouldn't be casually dismissed, but they're not your taskmaster either.

For instance, theological institutions, in the main, are in a fragile and weakening state. Enrollment shortfalls and budget constrictions are common, as are the low morale and the general sense of malaise that often accompanies them.

At Midwestern Seminary, we don't want to be normal—the normal seminary is in a death spiral. We intentionally eschew many of higher education's conventional norms. For example, we don't have tenure, we keep personnel expenses well below industry standards, and we intentionally operate well within our financial means.

When normal is doctrinal compromise, mission drift, plummeting enrollment, and financial shortfalls, why would we feel compelled to align with it? We don't.

As you'll see, we're committed to mission focus, extreme accountability, and keen stewardship. And these aren't just preferred distinctives; they are essentials.

Along these lines, I always think of Steve Jobs. He positioned Apple to buck the trends, to disregard conventional wisdom, and not to fear abnormality. That willingness became ingrained in Apple's DNA. And it made Apple all the better.

In Conclusion

To return to the opening illustration of ambiguity in foreign policy, while writing this chapter, I came across an article wherein George Will asserted the primary responsibility of the United States president, especially as it relates to foreign policy, is to "know his mind and to make it known."[3] Will recounted the occasion of President Harry Truman doing just that with the Soviet ambassador, and he encouraged President Biden to do the same with the current Russian foreign minister.

The ability to know one's mind and the willingness to make it known are needed skills for all who lead, not just U.S. presidents. And that's what I want for you.

At the personal level, I want you to have a settled awareness of who you are, what you believe, in which contexts you can serve with a clear conscience, and the convictions you're willing to fight for.

At the organizational level, I want you to put those convictions into action. You must lead, speak, hire, and direct in fulfillment of those convictions. If you're called to lead an organization, you're called to do just that.

And, at the operational level, I want you to lead with full conviction, even if doing that means you turn conventional wisdom on its head. Perhaps that's just what needs to happen to the conventional wisdom associated with your enterprise.

All of this is to say, lead on with full conviction and with the courage those convictions deserve. And as you do, you'll embody principle 2: hold your convictions.

3

Define Your Mission

It was my first trustee meeting to attend, and the board had one item of business: me. The presidential search committee had selected me as their nominee; now the full board of trustees would consider that nomination.

When all is well, trustee meetings tend to be relatively drama free, but in recent years Midwestern Seminary trustee meetings had been tense. This one had all the makings for the same.

I was thirty-five years old, short on executive experience but brimming with a sense of calling, and overflowing with naivete. I sat on the sidelines, watching as the trustees filed into the room at the appointed hour. They assembled to interview me and then vote on me as their next president.

They were a board divided, still simmering over circumstances surrounding the previous president's departure. They weren't sure what to make of the young man who sat before them. As the saying goes, you could've cut the tension in the air with a knife.

On paper, the schedule itself looked daunting. From early in the morning until late that evening, meetings filled the day. And I was the focus of most every one of them.

The meeting's location didn't help matters. It took place in a tired Embassy Suites hotel near the Kansas City airport. The rooms were cramped, the airflow insufficient, and the food awful. Purgatory would've been a more attractive place to gather.

Making matters worse, the lobby featured an enormous waterfall, whose sound echoed throughout the entire facility. The deafening falls necessitated raised voices for most every exchange, adding to the tension. By the end of the day, I had a migraine. I'm certain that waterfall intensified it.

The first item of business was to interview the presidential nominee. For better or worse, the future of any organization rests on who's elected to lead it. I felt as though the future of the seminary rested on how that interview went. That's because it did. More personally, I knew my future, too, was at stake.

There we sat, the full board of trustees, the interim president, and the seminary's legal counsel all together at the appointed hour. That's when the first skirmish broke out. The preexisting grievances came to the surface over a procedural matter unrelated to me.

That settled, we got down to business. The chairman of the presidential search committee introduced me, and I made my way to the podium. Seated before me, in an open U formation, were my interviewers. I cleared my throat and made my opening remarks. At last we were underway.

After my introductory reflections, a four-hour question-and-answer session ensued. It was thorough with no topic off limits. It was candid. Direct questions and direct answers. And it was . . . sweet, with all of us at the end of the four hours sensing God's affirmation in moving forward.

When the final vote was tallied, the results were twenty-nine to two in favor of my election. The two negatives later reflected they'd voted no out of protest of my predecessor's treatment, not their lack of support for me.

The Mission Moved the Needle

Plenary groups tend to affirm committee recommendations, but that's not always the case. I'd been subjected to six grueling weeks—from the time my nomination was made public until the day I was considered by the full board—of questions, criticism, and accusation. Many of the questions were fair, as were some of the criticisms, but some of the accusations were altogether off-the-wall. That's beside the point.

The point is that the board of trustees had been aggressively lobbied by interest groups, threatened by powerful individuals, and motivated to question every word that came out of my mouth. Though I'd submitted nearly forty pages of written documents, answering every question asked or anticipated, they were hungry for more.

This far outstripped the usual politicking that takes place around presidential elections. When a board interviews a chief executive officer, they have every cause to be thorough. This board doubly so. If I were in their place, I'd have done the same thing.

In the end, why did they take a chance on a thirty-five-year-old president? Why did I take a chance on this beleaguered institution? In the season that followed, why would team members join my new administration, donors support our work, and students enroll in record numbers?

The answer, I truly believe, is the mission I set before the board of trustees, and then, more broadly, our constituencies. It's three simple, but powerful, words: *for the church.*

Those three words are why we exist. They are our *raison d'être. For the church* is more than our mission *statement*—it's our mission.

In the last chapter, we showed how your convictions are your core beliefs, personally and organizationally. In the next chapter we'll unpack how your vision conveys where you're going. In this chapter, let's reflect on the meaning and power of the right mission statement: it declares why you exist.

And this is essential because every healthy organization knows why it exists, and every faithful leader gives visibility and volume to that mission.

For the Church

Over the past decade we've trumpeted our *for the church* mission as loudly as we can. It's been implemented across every square inch of the campus, embedded into every aspect of our institutional programming and curriculum, and embraced by every member of the team.

Moreover, *for the church* has given us institutional momentum. It's been an igniter, a propellant moving us forward, and it's galvanized our constituency to support us. It's been a cohesive, binding us together. We are *for the church*.

Ordinarily, a mission statement should not change with a new leader. Perhaps it's tweaked or reapplied, but it ought not be reinvented with each leadership change. In a sense, I was blessed because Midwestern Seminary had already been serving the church, but it had not expressed that mission in a clear, cogent way. I had the opportunity to clarify, to convey, and, every day since, to champion that mission.

When Winston Churchill was heralded as the lionhearted leader of wartime Great Britain, he famously said, "It was a nation and a race dwelling all around the globe that had the lion heart. I had the luck to be called upon to give the roar."[1]

I feel the same way toward Midwestern Seminary's *for the church* mission. Before me were faithful men and women already serving *for the church*. Yet, like Churchill, I've had the pleasure of articulating that mission and leveraging all the seminary's resources *for the church* in a way that hadn't been done before.

At the personal level, *for the church* had been building in my life for years. I had twin loves, the local church and theological education. In fact, that's why I'd been dually engaged in institutional and local-church settings for almost my entire adult life.

But the *for the church* mission is so much bigger and better than I am. It's not just autobiographical; it's biblical. Christ has promised to build His church, not His seminary. But as we're faithful to serve His church, we can know with confidence that we abide under His favor.

In fact, over the past ten years, I've watched with pleasure as *for the church* has gone from being *my* mission statement for Midwestern Seminary, to *our* mission statement for Midwestern Seminary, to *the* mission statement of Midwestern Seminary.

It animates our team, represents our institution, and inspires our constituency. Together, we are *for the church*.

Laying a New Foundation

Though Midwestern Seminary was oriented toward the church, we still had to lay a new foundation and build a new institutional superstructure on top of that foundation. Now everyone knows us by those ever-present three words; a decade ago, no one did.

As a case study, consider this article I penned early in my presidency. In it I set forth, for both internal stakeholders and external constituencies, our renewed mission. I also explain why we planted our standard there. Read it carefully, as we'll use it for a case study in identifying and communicating your organization's mission.[2]

In Arthur Schlesinger's award-winning biography of Franklin Roosevelt, he famously labeled the economic and political malaise of the 1930s as "the crisis of the old order." Schlesinger argued that political, cultural, and economic norms were changing so rapidly that, coupled with government inaction, they coalesced to form a crisis of the entire American status quo—a crisis that would upend society and necessitate a reenvisioning of American economic and social policy.

Observers of higher education likewise acknowledge a crisis exists in many seminaries and divinity schools. This crisis is so profound that it is forcing institutions to reconceptualize their model of education and their means of delivering it.

Admittedly, *crisis* is a tired word. We hear of political, economic, geopolitical, and cultural crises. Yet, when subjected to careful review, theological education in North America must be deemed as in a state of crisis. This current distress evidences itself in at least three areas.

First, most theological institutions in America find themselves, at least to some degree, mired in a crisis of resources. The escalating costs of higher education, nagging questions about the value of advanced degrees, encroaching federal regulations, and persistent economic sluggishness, present even the best-funded institutions with daunting operational challenges.

This crisis of resources has forced historic institutions to merge or close and has left the remaining ones searching for a sustainable business model. These financial realities, and more, have been like a spiraling whirlpool, drawing almost every theological institution into its vortex. The persistent generosity of Southern Baptists through the Cooperative Program has mitigated this challenge; however, even Southern Baptist seminaries are not immune to this struggle.

Sadly, the most urgent and consequential crisis in theological education is not one of funding. It is more fundamental and philosophical; the crisis is one of identity. What is a seminary to be? Stemming from and coupled with this crisis of identity is a crisis of mission. What is a seminary to do? Why does it exist?

The answers to these questions of identity and mission are predetermined because a seminary is to be a precommitted entity—looking to Scripture for its purpose and mission. When a seminary looks to Scripture for its identity, it will be drawn to one inescapable conclusion: a seminary must exist *for the church*.

When Christ promised in Matthew 16 to build His church, it was more than a reference to a secondary kingdom initiative. Rather, it was a prophetic word, a declaration, as to His redemptive and kingdom intent.

After all, Christ died for His church. He is the head of His church. He is the church's bridegroom. He gifts His followers for service in the church. He calls out pastors, teachers, and evangelists to equip His church. When baptized, believers are baptized into His church. Christ is currently building His church, and He will one day return for His church. In fact, Christ is so personalized with His church that He identifies persecution against His church as persecution of Himself.

Therefore, Christ's preoccupation with His church must inform a seminary's rationale and mission. His pledge to build His church is not only a promise to which a seminary should cling, but it is also a mandate a seminary should embrace. After all, Jesus has promised to build His church—not His seminary.

Though in the New Testament the form of a seminary is more overheard than heard, the function of a seminary— teaching, equipping, mentoring, and sending—is heard clearly. In many ways the entire trajectory and contour of the New Testament points to Christ fulfilling His promise to build His church. Moreover, the New Testament Epistles read like a veritable manual of how to do and how not to do church, conveying the predominant concern of health, growth, and faithfulness for the local church.

Cleavage between the seminary and the church is to the detriment of the former because it undermines its rationale for existence. That same cleavage also robs the church of further equipping for the work of ministry. If a seminary drifts from the church, the church will drift from it; if the seminary stops serving the church, the church will—and should—stop supporting it.

Of all denominations, the Southern Baptist Convention is uniquely positioned to enjoy seminaries that exist for the church. After all, the Southern Baptist Convention is nothing more than a confederation of churches, structured with a denominational framework that exists by, for, and as part of her churches.

By New Testament mandate, denominational expectation, and self-imposed determination, Midwestern Baptist Theological Seminary stands without compromise in its commitment to serve the local church. Thankfully, there is no question of identity or mission. Trustees and donors are not being polled to inform the identity of Midwestern Seminary. Focus groups are not being assembled and queried as to what our market niche should be. Faculty and students are not being surveyed to find our mission. On the contrary, with appropriate self-confidence, Midwestern Seminary is unquestionably committed to serving the church and is unapologetically bending her resources and energies toward this end.

This is not to suggest that other SBC seminaries or institutions beyond our denomination are not serving the church and not serving the church well. Nor is it to suggest that Midwestern Seminary in her past has not served the church and served it well.

This is to say that regardless of what other institutions are or are not doing and regardless of what Midwestern Seminary has or has not done, the future is certain: Midwestern Seminary exists *for the church*. Every proposed event, initiative, class, program, employee, or decision made will be subjugated to one overarching question: How will this help Midwestern Seminary fulfill its mission to serve the church?

For the church is a mission to be implemented over every square inch of Midwestern Seminary's campus, and it is a message to be carried to every corner of this great denomination. Midwestern Seminary's identity and mission are clear: Midwestern Seminary exists *for the church*.

Note what my article sought to accomplish. I not only gave *the why* of Midwestern Seminary (*for the church*), but I also gave *the why of the why*. I announced a mission, and I made the case for it. Also, note how mission and vision are a bit conflated. As I've stated, that's not ideal. But the truth is, I knew our mission from day one, but it would take many months to hammer out the shorter-term vision.

Define Your Mission

You must answer three questions about the entity you serve:

What do we believe?

Why do we exist?

Where are we going?

As stated earlier, an organization's mission statement ought to be perennial, not seasonal. It should endure, leader to leader, generation to generation. The deeper it's rooted in the organization's foundation, the taller it will stand, the farther it will project, and the longer it will endure.

Midwestern Seminary didn't poll donors to find out why we should exist. We didn't survey our student body to see what they wanted us to exist for. And we certainly didn't pore over research data to determine if *for the church* would find a suitable market niche.

No, we asked the big-picture, transcendent questions. Why did Southern Baptists start Midwestern Seminary? As a theological institution, we searched the Scriptures for clues on ministry preparation, pastoral training, and local-church service. More broadly, we reflected on the needs of the churches we serve. They need a new generation of pastors, ministers, and missionaries prepared *for the church*.

You also need to ask big-picture, transcendent questions and not rest until you have the big-picture, transcendent answers. Why was your organization founded? What are your core convictions and calling? How do you best serve the constituency you were established to serve?

Define Your Mission, Strengthen Your Leadership

Throughout this book you've sensed my dual focus. Primarily I'm writing to you, the leader. But I'm also writing to your organization. Those two tracks are not in conflict. In fact, they should be synergistic, strengthening each other. As you grow as a leader, your organization will benefit. Thus, in that spirit of interwovenness, consider how the right mission statement serves both you and those you lead.

It will unite your organization. The mission will draw you forward, magnetically pulling your team together. The clearer you are on your mission, the more potential employees will self-cull, not joining your team in the first place if they don't resonate with it. As you build your team, that common, animating motive brings you all together.

Or, as *Indeed*'s editorial team puts it: "When looking for a job, many people use a company's mission statement to decide if they want to apply. A strong mission statement that people can relate to encourages talented people to get involved with the company. Mission statements allow like-minded people with similar goals to naturally work together on projects that are most important to them."[3]

That's why, when it comes to personnel, you must communicate the mission. At the end of the day, every employee should be grounded in the mission for which they are working. Doing that for your team will be life-giving. So give your people the *why*. They crave it. It's like milk to a baby, red meat to a ravenous lion. Give them the *why!*

It will reassure your team. The mission reminds you that you exist for a higher purpose and will not be deterred by momentary setbacks. The mission is bigger than a down quarter, a disappointing initiative, or a cantankerous constituent. The mission also reminds you that it's bigger than a paycheck or some other fleeting opportunity. The mission reassures you—and, more important, your team—why you exist.

Along these lines, *Indeed*'s editorial team is again helpful: "A strong mission statement gives employees purpose and improves engagement in their work. Mission statements help employees see the meaning and purpose of their work by giving them clear reasons their job benefits a larger goal. Mission statements help employees see the positive aspects of their daily activities, boosting morale and creating long-term employee investment in the workplace culture."[4]

It will clarify your resourcing. The mission simplifies and clarifies not just why your organization exists, but also what it should do. As the saying goes: desperate times call for desperate measures. In organizational settings, desperate times often lead to mission drift. When money is tight, organizations often try long-shot endeavors that dilute their mission. They do so in pursuit of additional revenue streams. Before you know it, you may be engaged in activities far outside of your mission and your area of expertise.

Keeping the mission front and center will bring clarity to your initiative list, helping you avoid items that aren't mission critical. It will also serve as a circumference around your work, delineating what comports with your mission and what doesn't. What's more, it will simplify resource allocation.

As the human resources company MRA notes: "No organization has all the resources it could use, whether financial, environmental or human. Resource allocation decisions are among the hardest but linking those decisions to an organization's mission makes them more reasoned and defensible."[5]

It will shape your constituency. When rightly applied and communicated, your mission statement will shape those who are drawn to it. It's both a magnet and a repellent, for both internal and external persons. Leadership is a game of addition, not subtraction. But your organization will not be for everyone. And that's okay.

A clear mission statement will free you from the burden of trying to please those who do not align with your organization's mission. Some people will be upset that you've not made their mission your mission. Don't try to please the unpleasable. It's usually not worth the time and energy you'd spend trying to keep them on board.

So, through all this, remember the mission will help determine your constituency. Or, as I like to say, the organization determines the mission. Over time, the mission determines the organization, including the constituency it serves.

Lastly, it will rightly define success. Every employee—including the CEO—needs to know where the end zone is and how many yards they must go. Human impulse is to pursue temporal, pragmatic wins. The faithful leader will evaluate success in terms of convictional and mission faithfulness.

Amanda Ferenczy helpfully elaborates on this point:

A mission statement . . . provides the basis for judging the success of an organization and its goals. It helps the organization verify if it is on the right track and making the right decisions. It provides direction when the organization is tempted by distractions and forced to adapt to new demands. Attention to company mission helps the organization adhere to its primary purpose and serves as a touchstone for decision-making during times of conflict. With a strong mission statement in place, it is very easy to identify your goals, objectives, strategies, and tactics.[6]

In summary, the mission matters. Communicate it clearly. Speak it loudly. Say it frequently. The future of your organization and your credibility as a leader are at stake.

Different Questions, Same Answer

Through my tenure at Midwestern Seminary, we've worked to measure our success by mission fulfillment. But, at a deeper level, I believe our mission has generated our success. Stay with me.

Due to the many challenges confronting higher education, only a handful of institutions have grown over the past decade. Fewer still have grown appreciably. And the few who've experienced significant growth have garnered attention. Midwestern Seminary has been one such institution.

So much so, that Midwestern Seminary has been featured in several major news stories in recent years. In drafting those stories, the journalists often reach out to me to learn more about our growth. I'm asked questions like: "Have you revamped your admissions office?" "Did you rebrand the institution?" "Are you spending more on advertisement?"

My answer is always the same, but I can tell it leaves my interviewer wanting. But, before God, the best explanation I can give for Midwestern Seminary's success over the past decade is those three words: *for the church*.

In fact, *In Trust* recently published a major story on theological education. It found that only seven institutions have enjoyed consecutive growth during the past five years, and Midwestern Seminary topped their list. When asked why I believe we've grown, I pointed them back to those three words. "It's due to our mission," I said, "We're for the church."[7]

In Conclusion

As I conclude this chapter, my mind races back to a faculty interview I conducted years ago. We sought an established, senior biblical studies scholar. As I interviewed an accomplished candidate, I outlined what we needed in this professorship.

I said, "We're looking for a scholar who'll teach future ministers and will write books to resource pastors, especially as they prepare sermons." He said, "I want to work further upstream. I want to write books for other scholars to use who'll write books for pastors."

He is an accomplished scholar, a godly man with a noble mission. But our institutional mission didn't align with his personal mission. Thus, we didn't move forward. Do you see the importance of a carefully thought through and intentionally applied mission statement? It enables you to differentiate the good from the best, the possible from the necessary.

And that's integral to a mission statement—it not only defines what you do but what you don't do. Daily I receive proposals for new initiatives, requests for new budget allocations, and submittals for new positions. The possibilities before us are endless, and the requests that come before me are usually compelling, or they'd not have found their way to my desk.

So you and I must discipline ourselves to ask key questions. *Will this initiative help us fulfill our mission to exist for the church? Will this investment enable us to better serve the church? Is this person committed to serving the local church?*

This is to say, it's not enough to have the right mission. You must make decisions based on it. You must discipline yourself and your decisions in light of it. You must make hires, launch initiatives, and invest your resources accordingly. Not doing so will slowly but surely undermine your mission, and that must be avoided at all costs!

And you know this intuitively, don't you? Knowing your mission is key to most every avenue of life. It's doubly so for your realm of leadership. Why does your organization exist? What's the story of its founding? Its core beliefs? Its organizational DNA?

Seek until you find these answers. Don't settle for anything less than a clear, robust mission statement that tells every onlooker why you exist. In other words, define your mission.

4

Pursue the Vision

Newly elected seminary presidents ought not face a major accreditation review on their first day in the office. Nonetheless, that's just what greeted me on day one.

Midwestern Seminary's board of trustees had elected me president the previous month. Over the intervening weeks I'd shuttled from Louisville to Kansas City, trying to get my arms around the task before me.

My family and I moved to Kansas City the week of Thanksgiving. Most of our belongings remained in storage until the president's home on campus was ready to receive us. We kept the bare necessities close at hand and squeezed into a temporary apartment in campus housing. Relocated we were; settled we were not.

On the following Monday I bounced into the office, predawn, briefcase in hand, ready to face the new day and the new season of ministry before me. That day is etched in my memory not just because it was my first official day in the office, but because of the decennial accreditation review that greeted me.

For colleges and seminaries, accreditation is as serious as it gets. If one's accreditation is jeopardized, an avalanche of negative publicity comes with it. Potential students become skeptical, and current students become more difficult to retain.

If a seminary *loses* its accreditation, the consequences will be catastrophic. Sources of funding will be put at risk, including federal student aid. Reputational damage will be long-lasting even if full accreditation is soon restored.

At the time, Midwestern Seminary had two accrediting agencies (we've since added a third). The Higher Learning Commission accredits public and private, religious and secular institutions throughout the American Midwest. The Association of Theological Schools is the gold-standard accrediting agency for seminaries and divinity schools in North America. They accredit Midwestern Seminary and some three hundred similar institutions.[1]

Though an institution is in frequent contact with its accrediting agencies, under normal circumstances it only undergoes a major review every ten years, known as a decennial review.

And a major review it is.

Leading up to the decennial review, the institution conducts extensive self-studies, compiles documents, collates data, and works around the clock to ensure every "I" is dotted and every "T" is crossed. No one wants an accreditation review to go south, especially not a decennial review.

This entire process probably sounds tedious. That's because it is. It's easy to knock accrediting agencies, and some of that criticism is justified. But accrediting agencies provide an essential quality-control function: they certify the presence of industry-standard best practices, and they assure stakeholders that all is well.

The site visit itself lasts the better part of a week. The visiting team reviews the institution from top to bottom, inside and out. Colonoscopies are less invasive.

Complicating matters even more, their review contains an element of subjectivity. The site-visiting team *should* review an institution based on the standards set forth by the accrediting agency. But site visitors are human too. Their experiences, beliefs, and preferences show up, to a greater or lesser degree, with them.

For Midwestern Seminary, the outcome of that decennial site visit could hardly have been more serious.

Bad Timing for Me, Bad Timing for Midwestern Seminary

So this day—my first day in the office—I met with the site-visit team. My newness on the job and my relative youthfulness no doubt heightened my anxiety. But the anxiety I felt really didn't need heightening. It all seemed so daunting because it was. I could hardly have taken it more seriously.

As bad as the timing was for me, it was even worse for Midwestern Seminary. As I've elaborated on already, the seminary had been in a state of crisis. Trustee conflict, leadership challenges, financial exigencies, academic blunders, and more had played out publicly, with much of it covered in religious and secular press. All of this led to plummeting campus morale—something that's always on the site-visiting team's radar.

The seminary *looked* like an institution in crisis. The buildings were dilapidated and the grounds unkempt. The sidewalks were absolutely covered in goose poop. Yes, goose poop. Making matters worse, the seminary's courtesy car that shuttled the accrediting team was an absolute jalopy, an embarrassment from bumper to bumper. It all came together as a formula for disaster.

Vultures appeared to be circling over Kansas City, and these site-visit team members may well have been among their number. A miracle I prayed for because a miracle we needed.

Into the Conference Room We Go

We'd enjoyed a brief dinner the night before, but we all knew the main event was the next day. Their visit would begin with a three-hour session with me. Just the eight of us, alone, to talk about the state of the seminary. We were slated to begin in the appointed conference room on the north end of campus at 9:00 a.m., so off I went.

But first, the conference room. To call it a conference room is to insult conference rooms the world over. Our meeting space felt more like a closet. The windowless room was without life. The floors, walls, and ceilings were all a sterile, operating-room white. The walls were adorned with a few unmatching, crooked pictures. The table and chairs may or may not have come from the salvage yard, but that's where they should've been sent, *posthaste*.

If that wasn't enough, our meeting space had doubled as a small dining room over the years. The walls reeked of fried fish and oversmoked brisket. It was a depressing room, perhaps the perfect choice for a depressing meeting.

Over dinner the night before I'd gathered that six of the seven site-visiting team members most likely wouldn't resonate with who we were as an institution by way of conviction and mission. Again, their work is to be objective, but that fact, and the broader institutional context, prompted a foreboding sense to settle over me.

As I trekked to the north end of campus for the meeting, I rehearsed what I'd determined to share with them. I purposed to speak candidly about the seminary's recent past. I'd tell them they heard it was bad, but that wasn't the half of it. I'd unpack the financial woes, the board strife, academic shortcomings, the morale challenges, and everything else I knew to be wrong about the seminary.

I spoke with full throat. I did not mince words. Nor did I hedge on the difficulties of our institutional moment or the challenges that stood before us. To the best of my ability, I gave a full accounting of all I knew to be wrong and of all the work I knew we had to do.

But I didn't end there. I then pivoted to where we were going. At that juncture, I focused not so much on our convictions or our mission, but on our vision. I painted a verbal picture of where we purposed to go in the months ahead.

At the end of our time together, the chairwoman of the site-visit team announced to the team: "We all know this seminary has been through a lot, but this young man has a vision for its future. We need to help him move the institution toward that future."

The point of that story is not that I'm a compelling speaker. Sure, I did my best, but Winston Churchill didn't show up in the room that day. Rather, the point we can't miss is this: the vision, even more than its communicator, carried the day.

In that shoddy conference room before a chilly accreditation team, I learned that *a compelling vision is, indeed, compelling*. That day the vision saved me, and it may well have saved the institution.

From Conviction to Mission to Vision

In previous chapters we considered the importance of conviction and mission. We build upon those here, and we focus our attention on an organization's vision. These three—especially the latter two—are often confused. As far as importance, conviction supersedes the mission. And the mission supersedes the vision. But as a leader, you'll most likely shape the vision more than anything else.

That's because an organization's convictions and mission are usually fixed. They rarely, if ever, should be updated. They should be perennial, enduring leader to leader, generation to generation.

Vision, however, is more seasonal. It may well be updated based on a host of changing variables, including a new leadership team, new constituency needs, resource fluctuations, and other contextual dynamics. Additionally, an organization's vision often has time markers, clear benchmarks on which to measure health and accomplishment.

Leaders, even accomplished leaders, often conflate an organization's convictions with its mission and/or with its vision. Interchanging these terms isn't the unpardonable sin, but it is confusing. For the purposes of this book, we'll say, an organization's convictions are what it believes. Its mission is why it exists. Its vision is where it's going.

Again, your **convictions** *are what you believe, your* **mission** *is why you exist, and your* **vision** *is where you're going.* Together, these three coalesce to define and describe your organization's **identity**—*who it is.*

If such matters are unclear in your own mind, they'll be altogether confusing for those you lead. Thus, clarifying these terms in your own mind, and within your organization, will best serve all parties.

Crafting the Vision Statement

A good vision statement should work both externally and internally and should be both realistic and aspirational. Each one of these descriptors matters. Consider them with me.

External means the vision should speak *for* the organization *to* your constituencies. Over time, when people hear of the organization, they should think of the vision. And as they hear of the vision, they should think of the organization. So I convey our vision externally in denominational gatherings, prospective student events, donor dinners, and the like. I speak of our *for the church* mission most frequently, but when I speak more elaborately, I unpack our vision too.

Internal means the vision should speak for the organization to the team members. It daily reminds your team what they're pursuing. It keeps your team motivated and oriented in the right direction. And as they see you given to the vision, it will motivate them to do the same. Your followers will expect your passion for the vision to surpass theirs, but the vision should also impassion them.

Realistic means the vision should convey reality. Yes, you want it to be forward leaning, but it ought to resemble the organization you preside over and the apparent direction you're heading. Onlookers expect you to speak optimistically about your organization but not dishonestly. Be optimistic, but don't be in denial.

Aspirational means the vision communicates what you aim to accomplish. The vision statement ought to be stretching, requiring collective effort. Midwestern Seminary is a faith-based institution, and we want our vision statement to require *faith* in God by our team. As we strive toward our vision, we believe God—and His people—will strive with us. But it's a fact-based faith.

Here I resonate with Burton Nanus: "While vision is in a very real sense a dream, it is a special kind of dream built upon information and knowledge."[2] Or, as Daniel Burnham is reported to have poetically stated it: "Make no little plans. They have no magic to stir men's blood and probably in themselves will not be realized."[3]

As to the practicalities, keep it succinct and clear. Vision statements need not be longer than one sentence. Ideally, it's short enough for your team members to quickly state it and for your stakeholders to immediately recognize it.

And, whatever you do, make it clear. You don't want to spend your days explaining what your vision statement means and doesn't mean. A misunderstood vision statement is worse than no vision statement, so don't adopt one that necessitates explanation. Elaboration, yes. Explanation, no.

One final word. The vision statement will help you, the leader, stay focused. And as your team members—and potential team members—detect your commitment to the vision, it will both motivate and reassure them. When I'm out of sight, my team knows I'm not holed up somewhere updating my résumé. Rather, they know I'm somewhere working to advance the vision.

Employees aren't stupid—especially those who mean the most to your organization. If the leader's primary vision is feathering his own nest, his team members will sense that and make their own life decisions accordingly.

The Leader and the Vision

As you envision your own leadership assignment, you'll best honor stakeholders by including them in the process, especially your closest colleagues. In this way it's like the mission statement. It's best when the organizational conversation migrates from your vision to their vision, to *the* vision. But, if you're the primary leader, don't be shy about generating the initial thoughts or with the final form having your fingerprints on it.

You're leading the organization so it's entirely appropriate to think in personal terms about the vision statement. Your leadership should embolden your team; they should draw confidence from their confidence in you.

To help us grasp the importance of leading with vision, consider with me one of the all-time classic leadership books, *Spiritual Leadership* by J. Oswald Sanders. Sanders's book is a must-read for those in ministry, but it's helpful for all who lead, regardless of the context.

While serving in my first ministry role, I happened across *Spiritual Leadership*. I was immediately captivated, savoring every page. It spoke to my mind but also my heart. No doubt that's one reason it's a leadership classic. Sanders helps us at this point on the leader and vision. Read and reflect on his words:

> Vision involves foresight as well as insight. . . . A leader
> must be able to see the end results of the policies and
> methods he or she advocates. Responsible leadership

always looks ahead to see how policies will affect future generations.[4]

Vision involves optimism and hope. The pessimist sees difficulty in every opportunity. The optimist sees opportunity in every difficulty.[5]

Leaders take lessons from the past, but never sacrifice the future for the sake of mere continuity. People of vision gauge decisions on the future; the story of the past cannot be rewritten.[6]

A meaningful vision for any organization flows out of gathered information, a clear sense of values, and a compelling sense of the importance of the nature and purpose of the institution.[7]

The exhilarating thing about leadership is that you get to shape the vision. The sobering thing about leadership is that your constituency expects you to do just that. And it will be hard for you to fulfill your leadership assignment without a thoughtful, faithful, well-articulated vision statement.

Consider Midwestern Seminary

To move us from the abstract to the concrete, consider with me Midwestern Seminary's current vision statement. Over the past four years we've pursued our vision *to be the strongest seminary on the planet by 2022.* Note, we're not aspiring to be the largest or even the best. Although those are noble goals, those aren't our goals.

Though we're hovering near the top on the enrollment front and, I believe, we can make a case that we're the best, those aren't our animating goals. To aspire to be the largest might tempt us to compromise our convictions or our mission. What is more, seeking head-count growth often causes poor financial decisions that would compromise our long-term health.

To be the best has a different liability. It's too subjective, too opaque. After all, how can an institution really know if it's the best? Theological education doesn't crown an annual champion like sporting leagues.

No, our vision has been *to be the strongest seminary on the planet by 2022.* Five years ago, we outlined ten strategic priorities that, taken seriously and accomplished satisfactorily, would enable us to hit our mark. Here are those ten strategic priorities:

- Hold the right convictions: *Baptist Faith and Message*, Chicago Statement, Danvers Statement, Nashville Statement.
- Project the right mission: *for the church.*
- Strengthen the faculty through institutional support and new additions.
- Build a robust, sustainable business model.
- Maintain affordability for students.
- Cultivate constituency goodwill; be humble, servant-minded, and thankful.
- Preserve institutional agility.
- Construct appropriate campus amenities.
- Launch and grow Spurgeon College.
- Foster a healthy, cheerful, attractive campus community.

I won't unpack each of these strategic priorities, but we've hit or will hit each one in 2022. In addition to clarifying for our own team what we're targeting, these priorities determine where we'll invest our resources, whom we hire, what we initiate, and how we're progressing as an institution.

In concert with my ten-year anniversary, we'll unveil our next five-year vision in the fall of 2022. Some of these strategic priorities will remain, others will be subtracted, and surely new ones will be added. We're still working through all that will include, but we know our new five-year vision will be *Until Every Church Healthy*. Thus, our vision will be focused on the graduates we aim to produce and the churches they'll serve.

I should add an important word here. Though five-year increments are the conventional time frame for vision statements, don't be married to a half decade. Five years is an eternity in an organization's life, especially in our fast-paced world.

A recent article on theological education encouraged three-year windows and an openness to revision after eighteen months. Our strategic priorities each had a lengthened life cycle, making five years an appropriate time frame. What is more, since they're more priorities than plans, they've proven immune to momentary setbacks and unforeseen circumstances.

Along these lines, COVID-19 caused many institutions to ditch their vision statements and shelve their strategic plans because they were immediately irrelevant. Our vision statement, and the accompanying strategic priorities, didn't need to be updated. If anything, the pandemic made them more urgent.

Consider the Corporate World

Vision statements across organizations will vary in origin, purpose, and function. For some, the vision statement is nothing more than their mission statement put into action. For others, it contains targeted goals over a specific time frame. Still others convey concepts or values.

For instance, consider these concept-based vision statements that focus on a key concept the company intends to champion:

- **BBC:** "To be the most creative organization in the world"
- **Disney:** "To make people happy."

- **Google:** "To provide access to the world's information in one click"
- **IKEA:** "To create a better everyday life for the many people"
- **Instagram:** "Capture and share the world's moments"
- **Microsoft:** "To help people throughout the world realize their full potential"
- **Nike:** "To bring inspiration and innovation to every athlete in the world"
- **Shopify:** "To make commerce better for everyone"
- **Sony:** "To be a company that inspires and fulfills your curiosity"
- **TED:** "Spread ideas"
- **Tesla:** "To accelerate the world's transition to sustainable energy"
- **Uber:** "We ignite opportunity by setting the world in motion"
- **Whole Foods:** "To nourish people and the planet"

For another slate of examples, consider these quality-based vision statements that include the type of products or services the company hopes to provide as they grow. Quality-based vision statements can also relate to company culture and operations.

- **Amazon:** "Our vision is to be earth's most customer-centric company, where customers can find and discover anything they might want to buy online."
- **Ben & Jerry's:** "Making the best ice cream in the nicest possible way."
- **Ford:** "People working together as a lean, global enterprise to make people's lives better through automotive and mobility leadership."
- **McDonald's:** "To move with velocity to drive profitable growth and become an even better McDonald's serving more customers delicious food each day around the world."

- **Nordstrom:** "To serve our customers better, to always be relevant in their lives, and to form lifelong relationships."
- **Starbucks:** "To establish Starbucks as the premier purveyor of the finest coffee in the world while maintaining our uncompromising principles while we grow."
- **Zappos:** "To provide the best customer service possible. Deliver 'WOW' through service."[8]

Vision Leaks, So Communicate It Regularly

Institutions are dynamic. People come and go. What is more, many campus positions are filled by students or their spouses. That means graduation services, though glorious, also represent turnover. Literally, every all-employee meeting at Midwestern is a different gathering from the previous all-employee meeting.

It's my job to communicate why we exist, what we believe, and where we're going. Our convictions and mission are so clearly established that it's virtually impossible to get hired without a good sense of who we are. The shorter-term vision needs to be communicated more frequently.

Since the vision statement determines a host of other factors, communicating it isn't just good for morale; it's essential. Employees need frequent reminders why they serve and toward what ends their service is channeled.

Jonathan Parnell warns us: "Vision, no matter how clear, tends to rust over time. We need to hear it again and again."[9]

Don't Rush the Vision

One final word: don't rush the vision. I learned that lesson in my first pastorate. My first pastorate was an exhilarating, joy-filled experience. With my full-term wife days away from delivery, we unpacked our belongings and situated ourselves in the church-provided parsonage. All was so well, so right, so sweet.

At about that time a church member pressed me for my vision for the church's future. The truth is, I was just trying to unpack boxes, learn church members' names, situate my wife for a successful delivery, and not run off any congregants in the process.

I assured her that would come soon enough, but I first needed to get to know the church members and the community before articulating a new vision for the church. She mumbled a few more words of concern, then left altogether unsatisfied. The next week the church sign showcased a new Bible verse: "Where there is no vision, the people perish."[10]

Coincidence, you think? That's what I thought too. But as I tactfully inquired, I learned she kept the key to the church sign and updated it at her discretion.

That episode taught me a few lessons: some people are simply unreasonable; communicate a vision as soon as possible; and, lastly, don't let just anyone have a key to the church sign!

In Conclusion

I conclude this chapter by going back to that unseemly conference room on my first day on the job. As I reflect on that gathering and the favorable results we experienced, one last lesson comes to mind: *sometimes the leader carries the vision, but oftentimes the vision carries the leader.* That's exactly what happened with the accreditation site-visit team.

They weren't moved by my eloquence. I have little of that. They weren't gripped by my self-confidence. I had reason to doubt myself on that fall morning. And they sure weren't heartened by my executive experience. I had none. On that day, the vision I articulated carried me, and it's done so on numerous other occasions.

As for you, don't settle for a half-baked, ill-conceived vision. You'll spend your days trying to carry it. Be patient, be thoughtful, and be wise. Produce a vision that will carry your organization forward—and that will carry you forward when you need it most. Pursue the vision.

5

Cultivate Trustworthiness

George Shultz was once the twentieth century's leading statesman. He held numerous high-government offices, with his capstone position being Ronald Reagan's secretary of state from 1982 to 1989. Shultz was instrumental in Reagan's policy toward the Soviet Union, stated succinctly by Reagan as "We win. They lose."

The Reagan/Shultz approach to the Soviets included confrontation and rapprochement, public disagreement and principled dialogue. Ultimately, their strategy led to the collapse of the Soviet Union and the end of the Cold War.

Looking back, three words came to mark the Reagan/Shultz philosophy toward the Soviets: *trust* but verify. More broadly, Shultz reflected often on how essential trust is to any relationship, whether interpersonal or international.

Interestingly, Shultz's last published article—which appeared in December 2020 before he died a centenarian—was titled "Trust Is the Coin of the Realm." Shultz synthesized the lessons he'd learned over his hundred years of life, including his many decades of public service.[1] He learned the importance of trust as a boy, and that lesson was reinforced throughout his life. He wrote:

> I'm struck that there is one lesson that I learned early and have relearned over and over for a century. Put simply: "trust is the coin of the realm." When trust was in the room, whatever that room was—the family room, the schoolroom, the coach's room, the office room, the government room, or the military room—good things happened. When trust was not in the room, good things did not happen. Everything else is details.[2]

Shultz illustrated his statement by recounting episodes throughout his life that underscored the indispensability of trust. Yet, Shultz also spoke futuristically, pointing to the trust factor as indispensable for a new generation of leadership, relationships, and international diplomacy.

Shultz was spot-on, which is why trust appears throughout this book. Within this chapter, though, we'll focus our attention on this topic, and I'll challenge you to lead in a trustworthy manner, to demand the trustworthiness of those with whom you serve, and to cultivate trustworthiness within your organization, both internally and externally. Your leadership credibility and that of your organization depend on it.

America, We Have a Trust Problem

Our national moment includes a startling lack of trust. Internationally, other nations wonder whether they can trust America's word. Domestically, opinion-based journalism makes us wonder which news sources are trustworthy. Social media, of course, has exacerbated these challenges.

More heartbreakingly, leadership scandals, sexual abuse, overbearing behavior by the powerful, and much more make followers question their leaders in the for-profit as well as the nonprofit sectors. Even in the home, divorce often leaves children wondering which, if either, parent they can trust.

Most tragic of all are the high-profile scandals that rock churches when spiritual leaders live in ways that contradict their teachings or, more shockingly, take advantage of the vulnerable in their midst.

All of this is to say, our society has a trust problem. If you lead, you likely lead where there's a vacuum of trust. Nothing will inhibit your leadership more than letting it stay that way. Trust is essential to every healthy organization. It is indispensable to every healthy relationship.

Recent polling data from Pew Research confirms that America has a trust problem. This trust deficit runs both vertically and horizontally, indicating mistrust in our government and with our neighbors.

At the national level, more than two-thirds of Americans have little or no confidence in the federal government, while roughly the same number of Americans believe it is very important to repair the public's level of confidence in the federal government.[3]

Further, Pew notes, "About half of Americans (49%) link the decline in interpersonal trust to a belief that people are not as reliable as they used to be. Many ascribe shrinking trust to a political culture they believe is broken and spawns suspicion, even cynicism, about the ability of others to distinguish fact from fiction."[4]

Sadly, America's trust deficit has metastasized more than we might imagine, impacting not just our view of government but of our neighbors too: "Fully 71 percent think interpersonal confidence has worsened in the past twenty years. And about half (49%) think a major weight dragging down such trust is that Americans are not as reliable as they used to be."[5]

Pew's research goes deeper into our trust deficit, and we should go with it, by asking the why question. The 71 percent of Americans who believe there's been a decline in interpersonal trust were asked to name why they believe interpersonal confidence has fallen over the past generation. Of those who responded,

Forty-three percent of those who think interpersonal trust has deteriorated mention some kind of social ill as the cause of the decline in interpersonal trust. For instance, they attribute the decline to harmful social circumstances like the isolation and loneliness of some citizens (14%), personally harmful behavior like greed and dishonesty (11%), or persistent social ills such as crime, violence, drugs and scams (9%).[6]

Thankfully, most Americans recognize the problem and desire to see interpersonal trust restored. Of those surveyed, 93 percent thought restoring trust important, and "nearly six-in-ten (58%) believe it is very important to improve the level of confidence Americans have in each other, while another 35 percent feel it somewhat important to find ways to restore trust."[7]

Mr. President, Can We Trust You?

Though I was only thirty-five when I became president, I'd led enough to know I should expect trustworthiness from team members. I'd followed enough leaders to know those leaders had expected it of me.

However, entering the position, I didn't fully appreciate how important it was for me, as the newly installed president, to radiate trustworthiness in my own life. Sure, I knew that to be a leader worth following I couldn't be hypocritical, calling subordinates to serve one way while I served another. But I didn't sense how important it was to exude trustworthiness, even in the small things, to engender trustworthiness and reinforce its importance in my team. And I sure hadn't realized how essential the leader's trustworthiness was to inspire his team.

But as I argue in this book, leadership is always contextual. In my institutional context at that time, trustworthiness was doubly important. For those who served at Midwestern Seminary, the preceding years had been challenging. Institutional chaos, organizational conflict, and financial duress had adversely impacted most every employee. And, of course, that led to significant employee turnover and widespread discouragement among those who remained.

In fact, many of the institution's best employees had jumped at other opportunities, as one would expect. Those who remained were largely in two categories: (1) those who desired to be elsewhere but, for one reason or another, hadn't found a new job; and (2) those who felt such a strong sense of calling to Midwestern Seminary that they persisted despite the hardship. Both groups survived by putting their heads down and riding out the recurring storms.

This struck me in a unique way on one of my first days on the job. I was toiling away in my office, attending to several institutional urgencies. I opened my office door to make a request of a staff member, but they were gone. The lights were out. The blinds were closed. The doors were locked. Poof. They were gone.

The staff member had evidently left for the day. I glanced down at my watch. It was 4:35, just a few minutes after the 4:30 closing time. I wasn't expecting staff to work late that day, but I was surprised I didn't get the customary inquiry: "Dr. Allen, we're about to head out for the day, do you need anything before we go?"

My curiosity was piqued, so I walked down the main administrative hallway. Suite after suite, office after office, door after door, they were all closed for the day. Lights were off and doors were locked. The entire building had been shut down.

There were literally no signs of life—there was no one to be found. The feeling was almost surreal. The scene could've been taken from a zombie horror movie. Or worse, had there been a rapture, and I was the one left behind? I was alone in the building a mere five minutes after closing time.

I stood in the hallway thinking: *Did not a single person in the building need to work even a few minutes late today?* That struck me as peculiar, especially in the opening days of a new administration, when I was making data inquiries, report requests, and the like—not to mention that the instinct to put one's best foot forward usually occurs during the opening weeks of a new administration.

The next day I found myself in a conversation with our director of Human Resources. He would go on to serve in several different roles, including a four-year stint as my vice president for Administration.

I recounted the empty-building scenario I experienced the previous afternoon. He chuckled and said, "I know exactly what you mean. We joke that you better not be blocking the door at 4:30 or you'll be trampled."

I realized at that moment that we had a problem. Perhaps we had insufficiently committed employees. Perhaps we had some who were unmotivated. Or perhaps they were simply beleaguered by years of neglect and hardship.

Regardless of the reason, one thing was certain: they were uninspired, and it was my job to change the equation. They needed motivating, and I was called to be the motivator in chief.

Exuding personal trustworthiness would be key in this effort. They needed to see my commitment to the seminary and my commitment to them personally. They needed to find *me* trustworthy.

Practically and morally, you need to demonstrate your trustworthiness to your team. They want to believe in their leader, and you need them to believe in your leadership.

My team members then (and now) needed a leader they could trust. They needed a leader who was trust*worthy*. Your team needs the same. Your colleagues want the same.

Trustworthiness, Better than Loyalty

Let's think more intentionally about loyalty and trustworthiness. I want to begin by being crystal clear: trust is not loyalty. In fact, I studiously avoid the word *loyal* when I speak to organizational health, when I interview potential hires, and when I coach leaders on what to expect from their team.

Yes, in some contexts the word *loyal* and acts of loyalty are appropriate. After all, who wants to go into battle with disloyal comrades? Can you imagine being in a wartime bunker with someone disloyal? There's a reason traitors are executed.

Whether on the battlefield or in your backyard, no one wants to serve with a disloyal team member. Treachery is never acceptable, and you should work hard not to hire individuals prone to such. But there's more to this equation. Stay with me.

Demands for loyalty can drift into unhealthy interpersonal and organizational dynamics. Loyalty is important, but too often leaders—especially insecure ones—speak of absolute loyalty as the most important qualification for employment.

At Midwestern Seminary we speak of trustworthiness more than loyalty. There's a subtle but significant distinction. To demand loyalty prioritizes the commitment to loyalty over its natural causes. To demand loyalty insists on allegiance, *regardless of whether the other person, or the organization, merits such commitment.*

Trustworthiness is the opposite. Trustworthiness prioritizes the character, behavior patterns, discretion, responsibility, thoughtfulness, and follow-through that naturally cultivate loyalty in the first place. If these characteristics are present in both parties, loyalty usually takes care of itself.

That's why for organizational and interpersonal health, trustworthiness is better than loyalty. Let's take a closer look.

Defining and Describing Trustworthiness

When trust is in abundance, so is giving the benefit of the doubt. When trust is present, your relational and leadership capital are high. To trust someone is not just to believe them, but to believe *in* them. But if trustworthiness is the goal, how do you know when you've hit it?

Note carefully how we're thinking in two realms, or two circles: the personal and the organizational. The former exists within the latter. In other words, personal trustworthiness may not ensure organizational trustworthiness, but it's essential to it.

Stephen Covey helps us to think in both realms. First, for the personal, he writes:

> Simply put, trust means confidence. The opposite of trust is suspicion. When you trust people you have confidence in them, in their integrity, and in their abilities. When you distrust people, you are suspicious of them, of their integrity, their agendas, their capabilities, or their track records. It's that simple.[8]

Trustworthiness begins with the inner person, one's true character, convictions, and moral and ethical track record. But it extends to the outward, the practical. Yes, in organizational life, one's competence impacts one's trustworthiness.

Again, Covey helps us here: "Trust is a function of two things: character and competence. Character includes your integrity, your motive, and your intent with people. Competence includes your capabilities, your skills, your results, and your track record."[9]

Moving from the personal to the organizational, we see that trust is essential for every healthy team. I concur with Warren Bennis's assessment that "Trust is the lubrication that makes it possible for organizations to work."[10] That's why, "when trust abounds, processes tend to move more quickly, decisions are made and implemented more fluidly, and goals are met more rapidly."[11]

In fact, it's hard to outwork, out strategize, or out incentivize a deficit of trust. Distrust is sand in the gears. It's water in the gas tank. It's an insurmountable headwind, slowing all forward momentum. Trust is necessary for every lasting relationship, personal or organizational.

And where you find a trust problem, you'll most likely trace it back to a deeper, root problem. For example, consider an article in the *Harvard Business Review* on trust, what adds to it, and what depletes it.

> In our experience, trust has three core drivers: authenticity, logic, and empathy. People tend to trust you when they believe they are interacting with the real you (authenticity), when they have faith in your judgment and competence (logic), and when they feel that you care about them (empathy). When trust is lost, it can almost always be traced back to one of these three drivers.[12]

Trust, Necessary for Every Lasting Relationship

You know this intuitively to be true, don't you? A marriage that lacks trust is no marriage at all. A friendship deprived of trust will remain shallow, if it remains at all. Indeed, Stephen Covey is right, "Trust is the glue of life. It's the most essential ingredient in effective communication. It's the foundational principle that holds all relationships."[13]

Perhaps this, in part, is why our politics is so broken. Old Washingtonians recall the days when colleagues of different political parties would socialize, cultivating friendships and deepening their trust one with another. But today this seems increasingly rare.

Interpersonally, trust, once broken, is nearly impossible to fully restore. As I often remind my colleagues, trust sprints out of town but returns in a crawl.

Trust is also necessary for conflict resolution. Where there is an absence of trust, there will be an absence of healing. Sure, the conflict may scab over, but there'll be no real healing or any enduring relational health.

Developing Trustworthiness in Those You Lead

Now, let's move to the specific, the detailed. You need a trustworthy team around you. Until you have it, your leadership and your organization will be stymied. Trustworthiness isn't formulaic, but it is uncanny how the right, intentional steps lead to the right, desired outcomes. Here are a few steps I've found helpful:

1. *Hire the right people.* We cover this extensively in chapter 6, but if you detect untrustworthiness in the interview process, steer clear. Here it's key to evaluate past places of employment and how they speak of past employers. If someone has treachery in their DNA, you will not coax that out of them.

2. *Insist they not violate confidentialities.* On this point, I'm not so concerned about those who would intentionally violate a confidentiality because I'd deal with it head-on. I'm more concerned about those who do so through carelessness. I like to think out loud with colleagues. If I question a close colleague's ability to hold those conversations in confidence, I find myself unconsciously limiting those visits. So will you.

3. *Practice the seven-day window.* With my close colleagues, the seven-day window is a hard-and-fast rule. If I've given offense, they have seven days to raise it with me. I abide by the same principle with them. This keeps the accounts short, and it prevents issues from festering. I refuse to permit a culture of grievance to persist. If the offense isn't severe enough to merit a conversation, it must be let go. If it's so severe they can't let it go, then they must come to me to talk it through. This principle has served us well. It will serve you and your organization well too.

4. ***Insist they embrace personal accountability.*** If someone's reluctant for accountability, alarms bells go off in my head. That concern quickly metastasizes from the issue at hand to their broader character and job performance. Conversely, those who happily embrace accountability reassure me they're trustworthy.

5. ***Insist they not drop balls.*** You're not their administrative assistant, so don't play that role. They should work to always follow through and to never drop balls. Make clear, "Who will do what by when?" and insist they do it. Little things, like dropped balls, become big things over time.

6. ***Require clear, prompt communication.*** Subordinates should work to never surprise you. If they're wondering whether they should tell you something, that's a prompt to tell you immediately. If they're thinking through when and how to break the news to you, they should know to touch base with you *posthaste.* My team knows that I want more communication, not less. And that I want it sooner than later.

7. ***Be direct.*** Candid, direct communication is essential to trustworthiness. Don't make people live in purgatory, wondering what their boss really thinks of them. Such direct communication will boomerang back into greater trustworthiness.

Eliciting Trust from Those You Lead

As I mentioned, trustworthiness is a contextual reality, and it's a two-way street. Here are a few ways I've learned to deepen my own trustworthiness. These most likely will help you too.

1. ***Guard your character.*** To not do so is to forfeit your moral authority, which is essential for your own trustworthiness. The specific expectations will vary based on your context, but your people must see in you not only the expected character traits, but

more. They should perceive virtue, grace, and truthfulness, and find you altogether worthy of following.

2. ***Practice what you preach.*** We all preach a better game than we practice, but leaders must not, at their core, be hypocrites. Michael Holland argues: "Authentic leadership is revealed in the alignment of what you think, what you say, and what you do."[14] More to the point, practice the seven-day window, embrace accountability, and do not violate confidences.

3. ***Be all in.*** Your team should sense your commitment exceeds their own. That's the burden of leadership—you lead. You're out front. You're in the trenches. Your sacrificial effort inspires greater effort from others. Your employees should not sense they're propping you up so you can enjoy a semiretired lifestyle.

4. ***Acknowledge when you move the goalposts.*** Most every leader moves the goalposts. I know I do. However, I work to acknowledge it when I do. To move the goalposts is to delay organizational accomplishment and, for your employees, their personal achievement. That's a deflating environment in which to serve. When you move the goalposts, acknowledge you're doing it, celebrate the present achievement, and graciously point toward the revised goal.

5. ***Share the spoils of victory.*** Make sure your team knows that organizational victories lead to personal ones. Let the rising tide raise all ships, including theirs. The more your team senses you're committed to their future, the less time they'll spend worrying about it. Such commitment engenders interpersonal trust.

Trust, a Few Final Words

Leaders are coaches. And as a leader, I can't help but give you a few last words of coaching on this front. I'm doing so because I believe trustworthiness to be just that important. You won't have healthy relationships, nor will you have a healthy organization, without trust. Thus, consider these parting thoughts:.

1. ***Trust, you can't afford to lose it.*** The entity you serve is trust dependent. You must apply the practices we've reviewed at both the personal and the organizational level. And not just internally but externally. Potential partners want to know they can trust you. They *need* to know they can trust you. And *you* need them to know that.

2. ***Trust is a two-way street.*** The more you expect trustworthiness from those you lead, the more they should be able to expect it from you. For instance, over the years I've seen employers insist upon a time horizon of service—can you make a five-year commitment to this job? Perhaps what they're really saying is, "I want to bind your conscience for five years of service so that I can take you for granted over the next half-decade."

   This is to say, trust is mutually reinforcing. If subordinates trust you, they'll be more trustworthy. It's a mutually reinforcing circle of trust, one from which all parties benefit.

3. ***Trust is contextual.*** In your context of service, there will be organizational distinctives, and practicing those will enhance trust. It may be unique moral expectations or uncommon workplace policies. These may not be transcendent ethical standards, applicable to every organization and every interpersonal relationship, but if you've agreed to work there, they apply to you.

4. ***Trust is slowly earned but quickly lost.*** Or, as I said earlier, trust leaves town in a sprint but returns in a crawl. It's sobering to realize you can spend a lifetime accruing trust only to lose it by one scandalous act, or even something far less dramatic.

5. ***Trust isn't binary; it's a continuum.*** In most contexts, you will not have two classes of people, trustworthy or untrustworthy. Rather,

you'll have a continuum, from maximum to minimum trustworthiness. Trust is strengthened or weakened, enhanced or diminished. It can be earned and spent. It can be gained and forfeited.

In Conclusion

Trustworthiness isn't a switch to be flipped. It's a dial to be turned. Trust between individuals and within organizations is located on a continuum, and on the extreme ends are untrustworthy and airtight trust.

Airtight trust is not just that a person wouldn't intentionally break a confidence; it's that they won't break a confidence at all. Airtight trust doesn't mean that a person won't knowingly drop a ball; it means that they won't drop one at all. Airtight trust doesn't mean that one won't choose to follow through; it means that they always follow through.

Of course, no one bats a thousand. Accidents happen. All of us need grace on occasion, and all of us should be capable of extending it.

In other words, you want to place yourself in the airtight trustworthiness category or quickly trend that way. And you want the same for your associates, inside and outside your organization. In so doing, you must remember as you set about to create a high-trust culture that trust is a two-way street.

Coincidentally, while typing this chapter, I paused to work through my daily newspapers. In so doing, a story in the *New York Times* on the funeral service of Donald Rumsfeld caught my eye. Much like Shultz, Rumsfeld served in several high government positions, most memorably as President George W. Bush's secretary of defense during the Afghanistan War and the Second Gulf War.

As I read the proceedings from the funeral, Vice President Dick Cheney's eulogy caught my eye. Rumsfeld, while chief of staff to President Gerald Ford, discovered young Cheney and gave him his first opportunities in governmental service. Rumsfeld opened doors for Cheney that led him to high places, culminating in two terms as George W. Bush's vice president.

Pointedly, the *Times* article ended with Cheney's final reflection: "I had responsibilities and experiences far beyond anything I could ever have known. . . . He decided he could trust me, and it changed my life."[15] Indeed, the simple fact that Rumsfeld could trust Cheney changed his life and that of the country. Look for those in whom you can place your trust and hold them close. And don't forget, trust leaves town on horseback, but it returns on foot. Order your life so that doesn't happen to you. Coach your team so it doesn't happen to them. In short, cultivate trustworthiness.

Cherish Your Team

Every hire matters. It's one thing to believe that notionally. It's another thing to know it experientially. And I know it experientially: *every* hire matters.

Rewind with me back to Midwestern Seminary circa 2012. As you recall from the opening pages of this book, we found ourselves in a dire financial situation. Such that every hire mattered. The institution was broken, and nowhere was this more clearly seen than in our monthly financial statements. We not only had no surplus, but we also had no reserves and no near-term prospects of that changing.

I arrived with grand ambitions to build a first-class team. But how do you build your team when you have no money with which to build it? I'd led enough to know making good hires would be essential, but I didn't anticipate we'd have no money with which to do so.

What is more, the institution had been through so much trauma that I was reluctant to undertake widespread cuts to free up money. Besides, we were so thin that to cut risked slicing into the bone. Yes, we made some targeted changes, but those were the exception, not the norm.

During those early months, I learned that nothing focuses the attention like financial exigency. In those early years, we couldn't afford—literally!—to misfire on a single hire. Our mantra was *every hire matters.* And we stuck to it, whether it was for a dean or a groundskeeper, for a vice president or for a janitor. Every hire mattered then.

We still operate by that same principle—every hire matters—because . . . every hire matters.

The Firm

Over the years I've joked that we hire like the Firm, as depicted in the John Grisham novel by the same name. You may have read the book or seen the movie. The Firm was a small, Memphis-based law firm known as Bendini, Lambert, and Locke. They had only forty lawyers, and they were hyper-selective, to an evil degree, in screening those they brought on board.

The Firm was so selective because they were in bed with organized crime. They prescreened potential employees, hiring only those attorneys whom they believed would, eventually, go along with their criminal activities. They hired almost no one, but when they did, they couldn't have been more selective.

Though Midwestern Seminary stays on the up and up, in the early days we had to hire like the Firm, and these days we choose to do so. And I've never regretted it one bit.

We remain disciplined. With every vacancy, we ask ourselves: *Do we still need this position? Should it be combined with another position? Should we reallocate those funds to a more pressing personnel need or to a nonpersonnel need?*

If the position is still an institutional need, we seek the best person for the role. Why settle for less than God's best? We should never casually hire. We *must* never casually hire.

Every Hire Matters for You Too

Whether you realize it or not, every hire matters for you too. You can't outwork bad hires; you can't outrun disastrous ones. Bad hires usually take at least three years to get over: the first year to recognize it's not working out, the second year to undertake a transition, and the third year to get over the whole experiment.

Furthermore, at the moral level, we should be slow to dismiss someone because "they're not a good fit" or it "just isn't working." I'm amazed how casually some leaders will move a new employee (and their family) around the country, only to throw them overboard shortly thereafter. If the employee rightly represented himself, both sides bear culpability for a failure to thrive.

And whether you realize it or not, your organization—especially your organization's culture—is usually *not* made by the occasional high-profile hire. It's usually made by the sum of numerous low and mid-level hires that, in the aggregate, determine your success or failure. Yes, every hire matters.

In Washington, D.C., they say people *are* policy. If you want to know the course a new administration will set, don't listen to their talking points. Look to their personnel appointments. Who's their undersecretary of state or their deputy chief of staff? Who's been appointed solicitor general or secretary of defense?

The same is true for your organization. Your convictions, mission, and vision mean little if your team isn't committed to the same ends. The proof in your talking points is in your team. Do they embody these virtues? Do they share these convictions? Are they committed to the mission and vision? If not, your personnel will overrule your policy. They will undercut your mission.

When all is well, you might limp along with a broken team. But when challenges arise, that brokenness will surface. You'll not be able to cover over it, and you might not be able to survive it.

In the run-up to the Second Gulf War, Donald Rumsfeld famously said, "You go to war with the army you have, not the army you might want or wish to have at a later time." At the time, Rumsfeld faced media criticism for perceived deficiencies in manpower and equipment. His rebuttal offered an obvious but salient point. You have the team you have, not the one you wish you had.

It Takes a TEAM

When the word *team* is used in organizational theory, it most often refers to a leader's immediate, senior reports. You read of the CEO building her leadership team, of the new pastor selecting his ministry team, or of the new coach assembling his coaching team.

Yes, I also often use that phrase to refer to Midwestern Seminary's senior leaders, but to do so exclusively shortchanges the contributions of others, even those beyond the payroll.

Throughout this book I've told much of the Midwestern Seminary story in the first person. In that I'm the seminary's president, the book's author, and the one who's been privileged to lead here the past decade, that's fitting. But if you've not heard the consistent humming of the team, you've not listened well enough.

In fact, you'll recall that team is one of the four longitudinal themes that run throughout this book. That's largely been beneath the surface, but in this chapter it's above. And in this chapter, I want you to think, as I do, more expansively about the nature of the team.

In a real sense, at Midwestern Seminary the team includes all stakeholders, including those who don't draw a paycheck. Yes, we'll focus on how I seek to lead the senior leaders, but I don't want to rush by other essential contributors.

In addition to my office staff, I have three direct reports. In my early years I had eight, which is far too many. But in those early years I needed to get to know the institution and those who served it and to triage our most urgent needs and promising opportunities. Despite that, early on I communicated that I'd likely move to a smaller group of direct reports soon.

Now I have three direct reports and an executive cabinet, totaling eight. All eight of these are my team members. But, more broadly, so is the faculty, the rest of the administration, and in a real sense, every employee. But it doesn't end there.

Our trustees are also team members. Not only do they hold us accountable, but they also bring essential expertise to the table. In fact, informed, active, and engaged trustees have been essential to our success. I'm thankful for their many contributions. We have accountants who've strengthened our financial department, experienced contractors who've shepherded us through building projects, human resource professionals who've helped us on the personnel front, and strategic thinkers who've helped with master planning. The list goes on and on.

Lastly, donors have been incalculable. They've not only underwritten key initiatives, they've also resonated with our convictions and mission, and they've accelerated and expanded our vision. Supporters aren't just checkbooks; they're stakeholders. They're not morally obligated to support our work; they do so because they believe in us. And our relationship isn't—and shouldn't be—transactional; it is and should be personal.

Personnel Leadership Is Stewardship

Along these lines, you must realize that personnel leadership is a matter of organizational stewardship. For instance, essential to our institutional success is the team we've assembled. Every time employees join our team, they take a step of faith. Often, they leave a healthy place of service, moving their happy family hundreds of miles to begin a new life.

That's how it usually works, right? I'm not looking to hire someone else's malcontent.

To do so they must believe in me, my leadership, and my commitment to the institution. Similarly, they must share our beliefs, resonate with our mission, embrace our vision, and commit themselves to our institutional goals and future.

The leader plays a significant role in providing stability to his team. If I, as president, commit a moral failure such that I'm forced to resign, I inflict trauma not only on the institution I serve but also on the individuals, and their families, who've joined the team. Or less traumatically, if I depart for greener grass, that would be similarly disruptive. Think with me about the dominoes that would fall.

The seminary would be forced to find a new president. That new president would likely lead the institution in a different direction and will most likely shape his team differently. In other words, dramatic change would trickle throughout the entire organizational chart.

You get the picture, right? Regardless of what prompted it, my departure would adversely impact scores of employees and their families. On occasion, I reflect on this bleak scenario as a source of personal, moral accountability. I don't want to inflict hardship on the people I lead, nor should you—especially if you're a stewardship-minded leader.

Don't Rob Peter to Pay Paul

As to the team itself, don't rob Peter to pay Paul. I find it mystifying when an institution makes elective hires, creating unnecessary positions they don't need and can't afford. I find it doubly mystifying when they do so in a broader context of financial constraints. But I've seen it time and time again. They'll hire someone while simultaneously cutting benefits, withholding raises, and negatively impacting the entire workforce in other ways. Don't make unnecessary hires and penalize the entire workforce to pay for them. That's not good for morale.

Closer to home, I faced a similar circumstance at Midwestern Seminary. I'd been at the helm for several years, and we were making progress, but things were still financially lean.

An employee needed to be transitioned out. They insufficiently fulfilled their responsibilities and, making matters worse, to interact with them was to encounter sandpaper. That's to say, they lacked both competence and grace, and that's a bad combination.

The employee wasn't a direct report, but I'd had my distant concerns. Nonetheless, I had withheld judgment. One day their supervisor came to me, notifying me of his intent to initiate a transition. His assessment confirmed my observation. Though interpersonally difficult, institutionally it was clearly the right decision.

After we moved forward with the termination, a longtime seminary employee came to me to complain. He's a man I absolutely love, and the thoughts he shared with me are all too common. He said, "I know they're not really competent and that they rubbed people the wrong way, but it seems to me we could've hired someone over them to supervise them and avoided letting them go."

At that time, an across-the-board 2-percent pay raise for all of our employees cost the seminary about $120,000, almost the same price tag the new supervisor would've brought. We couldn't afford to do both, nor should we have done both.

When I responded to my beloved colleague that to create the position to retain that employee, as he suggested, I'd have to penalize every other hardworking, well-performing employee on campus, he got the message.

These same dynamics play out in organizations across America, especially in nonprofits. Lack of courage, fear of reprisals, or overwroughtness about personal disruption keeps many entities from dealing with pressing personnel problems. Over time, bloated payrolls emerge, ensuring everyone is underpaid. Keep your personnel house in order so you can rightly honor, financially, those to whom honor is due.

For instance, in the early months of the Covid-19 crisis and the economic disruption and unpredictability it brought, leaders were forced to live in budget-cutting mode. Yes, essential to that thinking was how budget adjustments, and accompanying personnel cuts, would adversely impact employees.

Those are dreadful thoughts to entertain, but they are necessary ones. The sign of a chief executive officer, however, is to be able to think beyond the individual, human concern to the collective, institutional one.

Thankfully, in the final analysis we did not have to forcibly eliminate any positions. But the exercise was essential.

A passive leader might forestall such deliberations, leaving insufficient time for prudent action if the worst-case projections prove accurate. Such an approach might have necessitated a meat cleaver, not the more appropriate scalpel.

Institutions are dynamic, not static. Unfortunately, it often takes a recession to force an organization to recalibrate to the vision it must now have, not the one it once had. To the resources it has, not the wishes it has.

Not Just on the Bus, But in the Right Seat

In his book *Good to Great*, Jim Collins famously offered the "bus" analogy.[1] He argued that great organizations don't just have the right people on the bus. They also have the right people in the right seats on the bus. You'll be none the better if you have the right people on the bus, but they're in the wrong seats.

A willingness to ask team members if they're flourishing in their current position is key. Cultivating an environment where they're comfortable giving an honest response is more so. I look back on how instrumental a few of those conversations have been. And all of that could only take place in a context of trust.

A culture of trust means employees can safely express that other, internal positions would interest them. If you see they're not a good fit, they probably already sense it—as do others in your organization. Don't be afraid to have strategic conversations and make adjustments in this regard.

Build Your Team Carefully

Before we move to how to cherish your team, let's briefly note how to assemble it. Over the years I've monitored the "Cs" in hiring. They're not unique to Midwestern Seminary, but they are essential to us.

First, start with **character**. If the person is wrong on the inside, they'll eventually be wrong on the outside. As a seminary, we have a heightened focus on character, as we should. Pay special note to how they talk. Jesus said that out of the mouth flows the abundance of the heart. If character isn't right, run.

Character is not a final consideration for me; it's a preliminary one. If I have concerns about their character, they're not getting out of the batter's box with me.

Second, look for **calling**. This is also heightened because we're a seminary. I ask myself: *Do they just want a job, or do they demonstrate a calling?* If they're willing to move to Kansas City just for a 20-percent pay raise, they'll quickly move again for the same.

Third, check their **convictions**. Yes, you guessed it, this too is heightened for us at Midwestern Seminary. The question is not whether they are willing to affirm our convictions, but whether they will *advocate* them. Are they willing to die for these truths, as we are?

Fourth, do they align with your organizational **culture**? For us, it goes back to those three words: *for the church*. But, more broadly, are they a good fit? Will they add to our joy factor or diminish it? As we like to say, will they happily wear the institutional jersey?

Fifth, of course **competency** is essential. Can they step into the position and excel? Will they strengthen the overall team or weaken it? Do they have the requisite training and experience for you to have confidence in their abilities? And, most especially, do they have a proven track record of accomplishment in this area?

Sixth, look for added **capabilities**. Beyond the specific position, are there other ways they will strengthen your organization? Do they bring added value? Can you envision them contributing to the overall project beyond the specifics of their position?

Whatever you do, be patient. I've occasionally regretted a hire I made. I've rarely regretted a hire I didn't make.

Cherish Your Team

This chapter isn't titled "Ride Your Team" or "Flog Your Team." It's not even called "Lead Your Team." This chapter is titled "Cherish Your Team." That's for a reason.

A healthy, happy, flourishing team is essential for the seminary's success. It's also essential for your organization's success.

Cherishing the team is morally right, but it's also practically beneficial. I strive, albeit imperfectly, to do just that. Here are several quick ways I've learned I can better cherish the team God has given me.

Lead them well.

Of course, a lot can be said on this point. But here I simply mean by letting them know what I'm thinking, what we're seeking to accomplish, and, especially, where we're heading. On this point, rightly sequencing conversations is key. If they're team members, they need to know the plays we're running, what the score is, what our record is, what teammates we may add, and the goals we're after.

Communicate clearly.

At this point, I mean more than the macro level. The need to not just hear you but to know you. Loop them in, copy them on emails. Give them courtesy FYIs. They won't get frustrated by too much communication, but they will by too little.

Hold them accountable.

If I put them in ethically fraught situations, I dishonor them and their families. But if I allow them to put themselves in such circumstances, I too dishonor them and their families. If I allow them to be distracted or to underperform, I permit them to hold back the rest of the team. Accountability is an act of love, so love your team by holding them accountable.

Give them room to grow.

I don't assess team members by how they performed five years ago. I assess them, and honor them, by how they perform now. Seek to sense their gifts, their desires, and the unique contributions they make to your organization.

Honor them.

Dishonoring an employee isn't the unpardonable sin, but it is an unforgettable one. When you must critique or correct someone, you can do so in a way that's not fundamentally dishonoring. Even at the procedural level, seek to honor them. I often ask: "How can I best honor you in this?" That question is always well received.

Compensate them well.

I refuse to ask myself what it will take, financially, to get someone here or to keep them. Resources are always limited, but we genuinely do our best for Midwestern Seminary employees. The more you think about their compensation, the less they'll have to. I don't want to lose team members because of a personal or institutional oversight. I don't want to unintentionally push someone away by insufficiently caring for them.

Customize my leadership of them.

By nature I'm more of a generalist. I can helpfully engage each of the seminary's three main divisions: administration, relations, and academics. And I can also, to a degree, customize my leadership of those who oversee those three areas. Depending on who the senior vice president is, their strengths, weaknesses, and current needs, I'll do my best to adapt and serve them as appropriate.

Go around them with integrity.

I reserve the right to go around my direct reports to theirs. That's appropriate. Senior vice presidents are senior vice presidents of the institution, not president of a third of it. I typically do this for the sake of efficiency. Perhaps I have a question about an area beneath them, or maybe I see an opportunity buried under them. But I do so with integrity, copying them on my communication and looping them in accordingly.

Encourage them to prioritize their family.

I don't make them feel like a second-class employee if they need to miss a meeting for one of their children's soccer games or voice recitals. Family friendliness does have limits, but we work hard to help our team prioritize their loved ones. Along these lines, think also of their spouse and children. What do they like? What do they need? How can you serve them?

Be an "upper" for them.

Walking into the president's office should never be too routine, but nor should it be dreaded. I want my team to anticipate our meetings, expecting to leave encouraged and empowered. I want to embolden them, not deflate them.

Appeal to authority sparingly.

My reports know I'm in charge. Your reports know the same thing. You don't need to remind them of it daily. Just because you can do something doesn't mean you should. Flex your organizational muscles only when necessary, but when you must, do so without apology.

Work harder than I expect them to work.

My team knows I'm devoted to the seminary. Yes, I demand a lot of them, but I demand more of myself. I'm not using them to prop me up; I'm partnering with them in a great, noble work, and I make sure they sense just that.

Celebrate their victories.

Be happy for them if their book outsells yours. Celebrate with them if God gives them a platform bigger than your own. Ultimately, that's a compliment to your organization and to you as the one who hired them. It's shortsighted to feel threatened by your team's achievements.

Acknowledge when I move the goalposts.

I routinely do this, as does most every driven leader. To not acknowledge it is demoralizing; it elicits a spirit of despair. I've found that to acknowledge it brings a smile, a laugh, and a here-we-go-again grin.

Let them know I believe in them.

Obviously, if you don't believe in your team members, you'll have to sort that out. As for me, I'm blessed. I not only believe my team, but *I believe in them.* I trust their instincts, I value their insights, I receive their counsel. I'm still responsible to oversee them, but I don't do so out of doubt or suspicion. Yes, we practice accountability, but I do so in the context of trust and confidence.

Keep short accounts.

My team knows I don't hold grudges. If something is on my mind, I'll speak it. If something needs to be changed, I'll insist upon it. They know that no news means no news; it doesn't mean I'm somewhere stewing about them.

Give them my time.

Love is spelled T-I-M-E. By making time for my team, they know I cherish them. I seek to be daily accessible, to maintain weekly meetings, and to have, at least annually, substantial retreats with them mixing in work and play. And here's the sweet irony: the more you give on these fronts, the more you'll get.

Love them when they leave.

Candidly, this is hard. One can't help but feel a touch of rejection. When a team member leaves, especially if their move appears lateral, it will sting a bit. But do your best to take the high road—it's less traveled.

Add to their number carefully.

You must realize that every new hire impacts your team as much as it impacts you. In fact, they'll likely impact your team more than they impact you. So do so with care.

In Conclusion

In what seems like a previous life, I played college basketball. I lived in a dorm with other athletes, on a floor with other team members. When my coach hosted a recruit, he always had him stay on the floor with the rest of the team.

As much as my coach desired to sign the best player, he realized he had to be a good fit. He'd say, "You guys are going to have to live with him. You need to want him on the team."

The same is true in organizations, including Midwestern Seminary. My colleagues don't have veto power over potential hires, but, in a real sense, they have that power *de facto*.

If a potential faculty hire won't fit with the rest of the instructional staff, we'll likely hold off. Similarly, if a potential executive cabinet addition would upend our chemistry, I'd most likely not risk the addition. I care too much about our existing team to risk it on a potential one.

Like a mystery, you must coordinate organizational structure, work patterns, personalities, and how these various dynamics come together symphonically to make a strong team. When a healthy team is humming along, the total product far outstrips its individual parts.

And, once again, when it comes to new hires, be patient. Never talk yourself into a hire. If you're not saying, "Heck yeah!," you should probably hold off. That's what I've done, and I truly believe I have a team that is second to none.

Is my team perfect? No. But are they perfect for me and Midwestern Seminary? Absolutely. And that has made all the difference.

Nurture your team. Cultivate their strengths. Forgive their shortfalls. Honor their families. In short, cherish your team.

7

Insist on Accountability

Organizational turning points are usually more detectable in hindsight than in real time. That's the case with the story I'm about to share. We didn't perceive it at the time, but it's one of the most institutionally consequential days of my tenure.

It was January 2015. I'd been in the job a little over two years. By now I'd assembled the leadership team, we were working well together, and the school was making forward progress. Better yet, we'd begun to experience real institutional wins, and we were hungry for more.

January days in Kansas City tend to be cold. This day was especially so. It was a gray, bone-chillingly cold day as our executive cabinet all loaded up in a couple of SUVS. We drove forty-five minutes west of campus to Lawrence, Kansas.

For the uninitiated, Lawrence is home to the University of Kansas. And, in many ways, Lawrence is basketball mecca. In fact, basketball's inventor, James A. Naismith, is buried in Lawrence, Kansas. The University of Kansas boasts the historic Phog Allen Fieldhouse, with its associated college basketball museum.

While in Lawrence, we visited Allen Fieldhouse. We toured the college basketball museum in the Booth Family Hall of Athletics. And, of course, we stopped by James Naismith's final resting place to pay our respects. But that's not why the trip was memorable. The trip is memorable, unforgettable in fact, because of what took place in our marathon work session. That work session proved to be an institutional turning point.

A colleague had mentioned that the University of Kansas had a conference center conducive for our retreat. It checked all the boxes. It was close enough to Kansas City to limit the commute but far enough away to get us out of town, removed from institutional and personal distractions. There were hotel rooms, a conference room, and their catering service could feed us while we worked. And since we were meeting in January, between semesters, the facility would be quiet.

On top of all that, since it was off-season and close by, our entire trip was relatively inexpensive—no small fact, given where we were in our institutional life cycle. Off to Lawrence we went.

From start to finish, our entire focus was on enrollment. I determined to lock us into the room and not leave until we, collectively, hammered out our enrollment goals for the next several academic years. Furthermore, we'd clarify precisely who would be responsible for what, how we'd resource them, and how we'd achieve those goals together.

Identify Your Push Goals

At Midwestern Seminary, our total enrollment goal is what we call a *push goal*. Hitting that goal means we will hit a collection of other goals, enabling us to carry out a host of other institutional initiatives. In fact, there are few problems in higher education that can't be solved by robust enrollment.

You see, few institutions are fully endowed. Most institutions are entirely, or at least partially, tuition dependent. That's the case with Midwestern. If a tuition-dependent institution gets enrollment wrong, few other things can make up for it. You can't fundraise your way out of an enrollment death spiral.

Thus, as it relates to the pragmatic, quantifiable aspects of an institution, competent enrollment management is priority number one.

To be clear, this doesn't mean ever-expanding enrollment growth is necessary, achievable, or even desired. That's not what I'm saying. Schools can have contracting enrollments but be healthy overall—if led well. In fact, a lot of healthy, financially viable institutions have contracting enrollments. Thus, we call it enrollment *management*, not enrollment growth. We'll explore this more in chapter 8.

But for Midwestern Seminary in 2014–2015, enrollment meant everything. We had to get it right; which is to say, we had to grow. We identified our main push goals for the next several years, then we moved to the more specific, program-by-program goals. In the semesters that followed, our growth accelerated. And as you'll see, it wasn't by chance.

Into the Room We Go

We entered the room and embarked on the marathon-of-all-marathons work sessions. To call it a *marathon* is to understate the duration of our session. In fact, it's become something of an institutional joke among insiders, almost folklore to those of us who were there.

It was the *retreat* from which we all returned *exhausted*. Other than the brief history-of-basketball tour we indulged in as we wrapped up our time away, it was all work and no play. And that's just what we needed.

We ordered our meals into that room. Our breaks were seldom and brief. Our communication with the outside world was all but nonexistent. So much so, I recall my wife texting me, inquiring: "Is everything okay?" By the end of our time together, our team members joked that we should've packed astronaut diapers.

What exactly did we do? We created what's come to be known at Midwestern Seminary as the Enrollment Tributary Report. We mapped out every single program we offered, we set enrollment goals associated with those degrees, we prioritized and allocated resources accordingly, and, most importantly, we put a name by every single line item.

Over the years, we've continually refined the Enrollment Tributary Report. We've ingrained ownership and accountability as deeply into the institution as possible. Every line has a name assigned to it, and every name has enrollment expectations associated with it.

For those who find their names on the Enrollment Tributary Report, the setting of enrollment goals is a collaborative process. The staff members don't just receive their goals; they help produce them. We expect every contributor to feel personal ownership for their line, to feel personal accountability for the goals on their line, and to sense personal accomplishment when they achieve their goals. Institutionally, our commitment is to resource these owners so they can hit their goals and to reward and celebrate them when they do.

Less directly, we work hard to engender institution-wide goals and responsibility as well. We want every seminary employee, including those positions that are only tangentially related to enrollment, to lean into enrollment. Every employee is an enrollment officer. It's that crucial.

Oh, and by the way, at the same time we were expanding our enrollment goals and more carefully detailing individual and institutional accountability within them, we were also significantly reviewing our degree and course offerings—culling underfilled classes, unnecessary courses, and underpopulated degree offerings.

That next fall we eliminated more than 25 percent of our class offerings but nonetheless saw 20 percent more hours taken. The tributary report we created in Lawrence combined with the curricular reset proved to be a true hinge point for the seminary that led to a massive leap forward in enrollment growth and internal efficiency. The two fundamentally reset the seminary's trajectory and business model. And along the way, we learned that small gains add up to big wins.

Small Gains Add Up to Big Wins

I still remember my college basketball coach hammering away that games are won and lost on every possession. Every possession matters. In fact, every aspect of every possession matters.

Most teams, my coach chided us, just play the game, periodically looking up at the scoreboard. Toward the end of the game, they look up to see how it turned out.

So it is with organizations. Failing organizations pay little attention to the markers of health, and when they do, it's typically retrospective, not prospective. It's downstream, not upstream. They review what happened; they don't plan out what they intend to make happen.

Keys to Organizational Accountability

At Midwestern Seminary, we've sought to ingrain accountability into every aspect of the institution's work. This includes the organizational and the personal, the procedural and the moral. In so doing, we've learned a few keys along the way. Track these carefully; each one matters.

Be Specific

Even for efforts that require all employees to support, you should still deputize someone as the accountable, if not the responsible, party. As they say, "It is not that one general is better than another, but that one general is better than two."[1]

Steve Jobs fanatically applied this principle at Apple. The accountable individual became known as the Directly Responsible Party, the DRP. If a new product was to be designed, it would have a DRP. If a project was undertaken, it had a DRP. And if a sales goal was set, it had a DRP.

This principle is true in the United States military as well. An order doesn't just float about amorphously without a clear sense of who issued it and who's to carry it out. Military equipment doesn't just float about, uninventoried, without accountable overseers assigned. And missions aren't undertaken without commanding officers clearly designated.

All of this points to an enduring leadership maxim: *if everyone does it, no one does it.* You must ensure specific lines of responsibility. You must be specific, clear, and unmistakable about who's responsible for what. That's why at the end of every meeting I ask myself: *Who will do what by when?* You should do the same.

Clarify Authority

Not only must you be clear about lines of responsibility; you must also be clear about lines of authority. Organizational charts matter. A little ambiguity about lines of reporting can lead to big problems down the road.

Insufficient accountability nearly always leads to underperformance, and it too often leads to tragedy. In hindsight, I don't regret ever having insisted on too much accountability for a person, but I do regret not ensuring enough.

Even the chief executive officer of your organization should have accountability. In fact, I've grown to not just accept but cherish the accountability of my trustee officers. I know they're committed to Midwestern Seminary, as I am. I also know they love me and my family.

In fact, they love me enough to tell me no, to offer me wise counsel, and to give me candid feedback.

Observant leaders realize that everyone is accountable to someone, and that's good. That's even true for the president of the United States. As Albert Mohler writes:

> The difference between a president of the United States and a medieval despot is the fact that a president has to face accountability, most importantly on Election Day. An American president sits atop one branch of government, not all three. At the same time, there is only one American at any given time who is the nation's chief executive and commander in chief of its military. The health and welfare of the nation depend on the president's fulfilling those responsibilities without apology. But the welfare and safety of the nation also depend upon the limitations placed even on the president of the United States. The faithful leader understands why this is so and knows that power is both indispensable and deadly. The stewardship of power is one of the greatest moral challenges any leader will ever face.[2]

Measure Progress

Every organization has tangible and intangible components. Often the intangible are the most important, but they're usually unmeasurable too. Just because everything can't be measured doesn't mean you can't measure some things. Midwestern Seminary has goals around every important, measurable aspect of the seminary's work. And we measure our progress frequently.

Don't just measure the macro performance. Measure in the micro as well, including individual performance. Unfortunately, not every employee will be equally motivated. Laziness is one sign of living in a fallen world. Most of that can be caught in the hiring process. Hire on provenness, not potential. Look for individuals who have a track record of accomplishment, not just the potential for it.

For others, the issue isn't laziness but distraction. Some employees become bored with their daily responsibilities. They drift into what they wish they were doing as opposed to what they're being paid to do. So measure progress. As Donald Rumsfeld noted: "If you can't measure it, you can't manage it."[3]

Inspect Meticulously

In leadership, you occasionally get what you expect; you consistently get what you inspect. Aspirational targets, generic goals, and blue-sky predictions will not cut it. Such aspirations rarely come to fruition when detached from concrete goals, appropriate resourcing, and specific follow-up inspection.

I carefully track all the key aspects of the seminary's performance. I track them meticulously not because I don't have confidence in their direct overseers, but because I do. If I lacked confidence in those leaders, I'd replace them. My belief in them means that I'm confident, if they're rightly led, we can achieve what we've set out to accomplish.

For us, such inspection includes most every measurable aspect of the institution.

Prioritize Facts over the Narrative

The narrative matters, but the facts matter more. I realized this early in my tenure at Midwestern Seminary. I inquired about a particular academic program, asking, "How's enrollment looking for the spring?" The response, "We're growing robustly."

An untrained ear will hear the positive commentary, be reassured, and move on to the next topic. But what exactly does "robust growth" mean? And who is positioned to determine what's robust and what's not?

Those personal, anecdotal assessments are best made by those charged with reviewing the numbers, not those charged with producing them.

My team knows that I prefer they provide the facts and let me provide the commentary. They produce the data, and I'll editorialize about what it means. That's also true when it comes to Midwestern Seminary's performance among institutions in our peer group.

Track Relative and Absolute Performance

I'm typing this chapter in December 2021. We've dealt with the COVID pandemic—the most disruptive force to hit higher education in generations—for some twenty months now. We've tracked our progress through COVID in both relative and absolute terms.

It matters, contextually, how we've managed our way through the pandemic relative to other institutions. If other schools in our peer group were down, on average, say 10 percent, but we were down only 2 percent, then, comparatively speaking, we might be thankful. We performed well in relative terms.

But the analysis doesn't end there. Even if you're down only 2 percent, you're still down. And in absolute terms, that may well have real consequences. You'll have to absorb that 2 percent in some way, by making up for it with increased revenues in other areas or by trimming your budget to offset your shortfall.

So relative performance helps fill in the contextual picture, but absolute performance, in measurable terms with fact-based data, indicates how you performed relative to your own institutional projections and expectations and what course correction may be needed in response.

Review the Numbers with the Mission in Mind

The mission of the organization should overlay every report. Why you exist colors every enrollment report, quarterly financial statement, and annual executive review.

For instance, if I were president of a missionary organization, my goal would not be to keep personnel expenses down but to get them up. In that setting the mission would be to send as many people as possible—not, like Midwestern Seminary, to equip as many students as faithfully and as efficiently as possible.

At Midwestern Seminary our work is much, much bigger than what Excel spreadsheets can indicate. I trust you've gathered that from previous chapters. Not to measure the measurable would be imprudent. But all that measuring must take place in a context of theological faithfulness and mission alignment.

Incentivize and Disincentivize Accordingly

You don't have to lead anything long to know that different team members will be motivated in different ways and by different things. The observant leader recognizes these dynamics and customizes how he leads the team around him.

The Scriptures teach us that it's right to give honor to whom honor is due. They also teach us that the elder who rules well is worthy of double honor.

Generally, our practice has been to award across-the-board cost-of-living raises with inflationary factors in mind and to bless, broadly, the entire team as they all contribute to the seminary's health. But, in addition to that, we give targeted pay raises and strategic bonuses. It would be unwise not to do so. It would also be unjust.

We don't want employees to sense they'll have to leave the institution to earn a higher wage. We want them to know their future here can be as bright as the seminary's future.

In summary, incentivize and disincentivize practices and outcomes accordingly. If you reward bad behavior, you'll get more of it. If you fail to reward the right practices and outcomes, you'll get less of it.

Foster Peer-to-Peer Accountability

One of the great joys of my life has been to coach my son's junior high basketball team. Coaching this age is a blast. They're old enough to take it seriously but young enough to be moldable.

One of my primary emphases is the concept of team. We work together, we lose together, and we win together. Also, they run together.

If one kid is late to practice, the entire team runs. If one kid is out of line, the entire team receives the discipline.

This creates peer-to-peer accountability, which is essential in athletics. It's one thing for the coach to enforce accountability; it's another thing for their teammates to do so. It brings the team together because they don't want to let one another down.

Organizations are similar. Leaders can bring only so much accountability. Fellow colleagues play an important, supplemental role. That helps prevent vocational distraction, personal underperformance, and moral failings.

Note how Patrick Lencioni drives home this point:

> Peer-to-peer accountability is the primary and most effective source of accountability on a leadership team. Most people assume that the leader of an executive team should be the primary source of accountability—and that's the norm in most unhealthy organizations—but it isn't efficient or practical, and it makes little sense.

When members of a team go to their leader whenever they see a peer deviate from a commitment that was made, they create a perfect environment for distraction and politics. Colleagues start to wonder who ratted them out, they get resentful of one another, and the team leader finds herself being constantly pulled into situations that could be more quickly and productively solved without her.

When team members know that their colleagues are truly committed to something, they can confront one another about issues without fearing defensiveness or backlash. After all, they're merely helping someone get back on track or seeking to clarify about something that doesn't seem right.[4]

Dial In on Resource Accountability

People tend to be looser with other people's money than their own. And some will play mental gymnastics to justify an organizational expense. Such gymnastics endangers their employment with the organization, but it also jeopardizes others around them. For the leader to tolerate it endangers the entire team. Even if the employee's conscience and your organization's policies are elastic, the IRS's aren't.

In his essay, "Financial Oversight and Budget Planning," Jon Wallace provides essential commentary. Read these several paragraphs carefully. Digest every word.

Some of the best advice I received as a new president was to embrace a transparent accountability for myself and those that make up the senior leadership team. Three principles that support this mutual accountability include:

1. Bad news first
2. Full disclosure
3. No surprises

If a president honors the leadership team with this kind of mutual transparency, then all areas of the organization can move strongly toward excellence, including finance.[5]

. . .

Good financial oversight includes formal processes, procedures, and structures that ensure the organization has the necessary qualified financial staff to handle its finances, that funds are handled properly, that an effective annual budget process unfolds, and that income and expenses are monitored on a regular basis.[6]

. . .

Christian institutions and organizations should strive to be the best examples of decision-making that supports the budget process, financial management, and wise stewardship. I believe this means building appropriate reserves and contingencies into every budget. This gives both the leader and the organization a margin of financial protection against uncertain future outcomes. . . . Every budget and forward-looking financial plan should contain some measure of savings to grow your reserves to remain healthy against an uncertain future.[7]

The issue is not just whether the expense is technically permissible. The issue is whether the expense is good stewardship, especially considering past investments, current opportunities, and probable future needs. You must think generationally about your stewardship, not just momentarily.

Theological and Moral Accountability

Though in previous chapters we've explored theological and moral accountability, we should revisit them briefly here. First, know the ultimate act of love is to hold your team accountable in these areas where a transgression could be a mortal blow. In my context, a seminary, there are no bolder redlines than the moral, including the sexual.

The leader must be alert to these dangers in his own life but also in those around him. On this point, we look again to J. Oswald Sanders, who writes:

> Moral principles common to the Christian life are under constant, subtle attack, and none more so than sexual faithfulness. The Christian leader must be blameless on this vital and often unpopular point. Faithfulness to one marriage partner is the biblical norm. The spiritual leader should be a man of unchallengeable morality.[8]

Along these lines, you best serve your team by dealing with issues—be they theological, moral, or operational—before they become fully formed. The farther upstream you sense a concern, the more pastoral you can be in dealing with it. The more the concern has grown, the more prophetic you'll need to be. Catching the concern in early iterations is essential.

Some leaders wait until the issue has become public, then swoop in to play whack-a-mole. That serves no one well. Over time, it will undermine your own leadership. In the meantime, it will position you to be unnecessarily harsh with an employee, leaving them deflated and defeated.

Closer to home, I operate with a high level of accountability with my wife and family. I don't travel needlessly, nor do I unnecessarily extend trips. The seminary ensures I don't travel alone, and I fastidiously apply the Billy Graham rule of not being alone with members of the opposite sex.

Lastly, I just don't have chunks of unallocated time. My wife and/or my office staff know where I am most every minute of the day, and I've never once regretted that. I enjoy being productive, and that also cuts down on the probability of immoral activity. As they say, idle hands are the devil's workshop.

Even as I type these words, I do so with fear and trepidation. No minister ever awoke one day thinking, *Today is the day I'm going to violate the moral and spiritual qualifications for my office.* We must be—I must be!—ever vigilant in this regard.

In Conclusion

Let's end this chapter by reminding ourselves of the beauty in accountability. Accountability is God given, it's for our own good, and it's essential for health in most every area of life.

If you sense a team member chafing at accountability, that should be a cause for concern. If you sense yourself chafing at accountability, that's a cause for greater concern.

At the personal level, over the years I've grown to not just accept accountability but to delight in it. God has brought accountability into my life for my own good. It's liberating for me to be able to say things like, "My trustees have instructed me not to do that," or, "The seminary has a policy that precludes that," or, "We've made it a practice to avoid that."

So it will be with you. The more deeply you engrain accountability into the life of your organization, the more it will flourish. The more wholeheartedly you embrace personal accountability, the more you'll flourish. Insist on accountability.

8

Steward Your Money

Scripture teaches us: "Where there is no vision, the people perish" (Prov. 29:18 KJV). Experience has taught me, "Where there is no money, the vision will perish." Yes, money tends to follow vision. But if the money doesn't follow, the vision dries up.

In fact, I often say the job of a seminary president comes down to two words: *mission* and *money*. As to the mission, I must recruit and retain the right people who will enable us to recruit and retain students, all motivated to fulfill our mission to be *for the church*. What we believe and teach, who we hire, the events we hold, the initiatives we launch, and the graduates we produce are all shaped by one word: *mission*.

The second word, *money*, follows closely. Without money, we can't hire the right people, host helpful events, launch attractive initiatives, or produce the most promising graduates. Money enables these ends, but I don't just mean revenue. It's not enough to have money coming in the front door; you must steward it for organizational health—for the present *and the future*.

Where found, money is an accelerant, giving the vision speed and direction. And just as we protect and preserve the vision, so we must protect and preserve the money. In a word, we must *steward* it.

Stewardship as a Biblical Theme, Financial Focus

Stewardship is a common biblical theme. From stewarding our time and gifts to our relationships and money, stewardship is ubiquitous in the Bible. Perhaps the most-cited New Testament passage on stewardship is Jesus's parable of the talents. Even nonbelievers are familiar with this classic tale.

Jesus told His disciples:

For it will be like a man going on a journey, who called his servants and entrusted to them his property. To one he gave five talents, to another two, to another one, to each according to his ability. Then he went away. He who had received the five talents went at once and traded with them, and he made five talents more. So also he who had the two talents made two talents more. But he who had received the one talent went and dug in the ground and hid his master's money. Now after a long time the master of those servants came and settled accounts with them. And he who had received the five talents came forward, bringing five talents more, saying, "Master, you delivered to me five talents; here, I have made five talents more." His master said to him, "Well done, good and faithful servant. You have been faithful over a little; I will set you over much. Enter into the joy of your master." And he also who had the two talents came forward, saying, "Master, you delivered to me two talents; here, I have made two talents more." His master said to him, "Well done, good and faithful servant. You have been faithful over a little; I will set you over much. Enter into the joy of your master." He also who had received the one talent came forward, saying, "Master, I knew you to be a hard man, reaping where you did not sow, and gathering where you scattered no seed, so I was afraid, and I went and hid your talent in the ground. Here, you have what is yours." But his master answered him, "You wicked and slothful servant! You knew that I reap where I have not sown and gather where I scattered no seed? Then you ought to have invested my money with the bankers, and at my coming I should have received what was my own with interest. So take the talent from him and give it to him who has the ten talents. For to everyone who has will more be given, and he will have an abundance. But from the one who has not, even what he has will be taken away. And cast the worthless servant into the outer darkness. In that place there will be weeping and gnashing of teeth." (Matt. 25:14–30 ESV)

In this parable, Jesus focuses on His disciples' stewardship as they await His second coming. Each servant was entrusted with talents (i.e., money), and each servant was held accountable for how he stewarded his master's money during his absence.

Jesus's parable reminds us that stewardship matters to God, and according to the Bible, it should to us too. We are all stewards. The big question is whether we are faithful.

But we also sense this from common grace, don't we? We need doctors to steward their intellectual abilities for our physical well-being. We appreciate the uber-wealthy channeling their resources toward philanthropic ends. Parents should steward their life-shaping influence over their children. Stewardship matters in every area of life, for all of life.

Therefore, we should view every area of life through the prism of stewardship, but this is especially true of money. Many of us think of stewardship as primarily, if not exclusively, a *personal act*. That's certainly important, but that's not where it ends. Nor is it the focus of this chapter.

Here we'll focus not on the personal but the organizational. Not the individual but the collective. Stay with me.

Financial Exigency, Financial Breakthroughs

In the introduction to this book, I outlined four longitudinal themes that run throughout. As you'll recall, one of those themes is God's kind providence. Never has that proven truer than in relation to Midwestern Seminary's financial developments.

Lest you think I'm overstating this, review with me five financial breakthroughs we experienced, each one a sign of God's remarkable provision. But first, let me remind you where we stood financially in 2012.

In the fall of 2012, the seminary was impoverished. The previous year's budget was nearly $9 million, but the seminary had taken in closer to $8 million. Complicating matters further, the day I took office the trustees approved a second motion, one that seemed small at the time— to borrow $1 million to complete a stalled-out building project.

In the world of higher education, one million dollars isn't a lot of money. But when you're institutionally broke, it sounds like a billion. What's more, the loan had to be paid in full within three years. When I inquired about the seminary's reserve funds, our director of accounting informed me those had been exhausted years before. My concern was piqued.

I daily thought about paying the bills. When I made time to think about the seminary's finances more broadly, my mind always went straight to the million-dollar loan. Goliath stood before me. Managing cash flow with an impending debt crisis looming is no way to live.

About that time we experienced our *first financial breakthrough*. I found myself in Oklahoma City, visiting over lunch with a former trustee who had given much of his time and money to the seminary over the years.

While sorting his salad, he said to me, "Jason, what needs does the seminary have? I want to help, and I'm the kind of guy that will give to things most people won't give to. I'm even willing to pay off someone else's debt."

I could hardly contain myself. I responded, "You're just the man I've been looking for." In the months that followed, the debt was gone. We'd been set free.

Eliminating the institution's indebtedness was huge, but even still, we were running metal on metal. We had no financial margin whatsoever. We were one bad day away from returning to indebtedness. About this time, still in my first year, we received our *second financial breakthrough*.

A quiet, reserved couple gave an unrestricted $500,000 gift to the seminary. They lived nearly a thousand miles from Kansas City and had never been close to setting foot on campus. In fact, they knew little of the institution, other than that we were seeking to turn the school around and were in a season of great financial need. Their gift was perfectly timed, like manna from heaven.

Their gift was fuel for the seminary's engine. The money enabled us to make a couple of strategic hires and establish a reserve account. The debt had been eliminated, and now we had a little margin. At last, I could sleep a little softer.

While the first gift eliminated our debt and the second gift gave us breathing room, the *third financial breakthrough* propelled us forward. As owner of Charles Spurgeon's Library, the seminary had a singular opportunity. I knew we had to make the most of it. Let me explain.

About a decade before, the seminary had acquired more than six thousand books and artifacts previously owned by the Victorian preacher Charles Spurgeon. If you're unfamiliar with Charles Spurgeon, think of him as the nineteenth century's Billy Graham.

Spurgeon enjoyed a global ministry. He was the most recognized and influential minister in the world during the Victorian Era. In fact, many consider him to be the greatest preacher who's ever lived. Though he was born nearly two centuries ago, he's consistently recognized as one of the most beloved ministers ever, even by contemporary preachers. That's why we desperately needed a facility to house his library.

The total project was slated to cost $2.5 million, and we didn't have a penny to go toward it. Dear friends, whom God had financially blessed, indicated interest in supporting the project. I articulated my dream for the Spurgeon Library and sheepishly conveyed the price tag. I hoped they'd agree to contribute a portion of that. Perhaps they'd give a large, leading gift.

I still recall where I was, seated in my home office, when they called to say they wanted to fund the project—in its entirety. My emotions still stir when I think of that phone call and of their gift. It was a true game changer for Midwestern Seminary.

The *fourth financial breakthrough* came out of the blue. We were now in year three. We were beginning to crawl financially but still had shards of glass in our knees. Out of the blue we received an unsolicited one-million-dollar gift.

When I received the phone call, I was in Branson with my family. I know, I know. When you hear Branson, you think of Elvis impersonators and similar senior-adult attractions. But nestled in the Ozark Mountains and on the stunning Table Rock Lake, Branson is a great place to take your family. And the Allen family was there enjoying a much-needed few days together.

It was a chilly, rainy day. I stepped out of a movie to take a phone call from my office. They indicated that we received a one-million-dollar undesignated check in the mail. It was an unsolicited, unexpected gift. The donor had no previous ties to Midwestern Seminary. I'd met the family head in passing, but had neither requested nor anticipated a gift. This gift led to our *fifth financial breakthrough*.

We were now in year four and dreaming that God would give us the resources to build a new student center. Our enrollment had by now exploded, and we needed a place for our community to gather.

To say we had an amenity deficit is to insult schools with amenity deficits. We had no cafeteria, formal event space, gymnasium, exercise space, or recreational areas. Our need was great, and to step forward as a mature institution, we simply had to secure funding for such a student center.

The $13 million price tag for the proposed facility seemed altogether out of reach. We determined to avoid indebtedness, thus narrowing our options. As we reflected and prayed, it seemed that God was leading us back to the same family that had recently mailed in the million-dollar unsolicited gift.

Full of prayer and hopefulness, a colleague and I drove to Oklahoma to present to this same family the dream for a new student center. Situated around their kitchen table and having enjoyed a sumptuous meal prepared by the family matriarch, I presented the plans for the new student center. I asked them to pray with us, to dream with us, and to consider making a $7 million lead gift. Hearts were shared, tears were shed, and it all seemed so right.

We returned to Kansas City to pray, expecting to hear from the family within a month. I told them I only wanted a yes if they could do so with peace of mind that it was the right decision and with a heart of joy as they did so. About a month later, I was in my home office when I received the call from the family patriarch. They were in.

Do you see the theme here? With God, one plus one often equals five. Even as I type this chapter, I'm struck by God's continued faithfulness. Such unexpected, kind providence can be future altering (or, in our case, institutionally saving), but we ought not *plan* to need financial Hail Marys.

As key as these fundraising wins have been, we've worked hard to build an institution less dependent on fundraising with each passing year. To receive such gifts is to be blessed; to plan to need such gifts is to be irresponsible.

The basic, predictable revenue streams should underwrite the basic, predictable bills of the organization. I've told my board of trustees that if I bring them a budget dependent on heroic fundraising to meet essential operating needs, they should fire me. If they passed a budget dependent on the same, I should resign.

All of this is to say, you need to build a sustainable business model. Let's review what that entails.

Build Your Business Model

Every organization should have a business model—a template that projects the sources of revenue, amounts needed, and where to allocate resources. A business model includes a budget, but it's more than a budget. It's also a financial forecast, a commitment to your vision, and a statement about organizational values and direction.

In a sense, a business model is a convictional document, indicating what you believe. It's a vision document, indicating where you are going. It's a mission statement, determining where and how resources will be invested. It also aids the master plan, determining what the organization is pursuing, what resources it will have to achieve it, and how it will allocate the financial gains achievement will provide.

I recall sorting out Midwestern Seminary's financial reality in my early months, cobbling together resources to pay our bills, and dreaming about what a healthy business model might look like. Those original formulations were more aspirational than actual. But the discipline was crucial.

In fact, my first enrollment dream was to enroll two thousand students by 2020. That goal was not based on anything empirical within our enrollment data, but because I thought two thousand students was essential for a sustainable business model.

To be clear, the type of organization you lead will determine the nature of your business model. For instance, I work hard to keep our personnel costs under 50 percent of institutional expenditures. However, if I were president of a missionary-sending organization, my goal would be to make the percentage of employees as high as possible. A large workforce wouldn't hinder our mission; it would be mission critical.

I think you get the picture. Regardless of where you lead, planning a sustainable business model, and then hustling to make it a reality, should be at the top of every leader's to-do list.

Know Your Revenue Streams

To have resources to steward, you must have revenue. But it's not enough simply to have revenue streams. You need to know them. From where and whom do your resources come? How predictable are they? How severely will an economic recession impact them? For Midwestern Seminary, we have essentially five revenue sources.

Since our founding in 1957, Southern Baptist churches have generously sent us their money, not just their young men and women for training. In the early years of our existence, that financial support totaled more than 90 percent of the seminary's annual revenue.

Established in the 1920s, over the past century *The Cooperative Program* has proven to be genius in providing a consistent source of financial support and accompanying accountability for the denomination's entities and mission boards. Previously, each ministry solicited churches directly and competed for funding. This method proved insufficient in resourcing and never-ending in work.

The Cooperative Program called for each church to forward a percentage of their offering-plate collections on to state mission partners and then on to the national convention for distribution to the respective ministries.

The Cooperative Program has proven remarkably successful, funding the largest seminaries and mission boards in the Protestant world, and putting Southern Baptist entities in an enviable position.

Over the years, as the seminary developed other sources of revenue, the Cooperative Program has supplied less of a percentage of our annual budget. At the time of my writing, the Cooperative Program comprises about 25 percent.

Due to our enrollment growth, *tuition and fees* account for over 60 percent of our annual revenues. We work hard to keep our tuition and fees low, so our tuition growth is more attributed to enrollment gains than price hikes.

The final three sources are all relatively small and combine for about 15 percent of our budget. They are *auxiliary services* (things like room and board), a *modest endowment*, and *undesignated gifts*.

As for you, what are your revenue streams? How predictable are they? How vulnerable are they to economic downturns, hard-to-please donors, or a potentially disenchanted constituency? These considerations are not just important for managerial reasons; they're important for convictional ones.

Just as businesses work to please their customers, nonprofits work to please their supporters. Just as plants naturally grow toward sunlight, so organizations naturally bend toward their funding sources. Thus, for example, the Cooperative Program is not only an ongoing source of support but also an ongoing source of accountability. This accountability extends to our convictions and our mission.

Therefore, to come full circle, the faithful leader doesn't make an annual assessment of financial needs and then adjust the organization's beliefs and mission to find willing supporters. To do so is treachery, especially if one considers the long history of past support.

Track Your Bills Closely

More important than knowing your revenue sources, you must know your bills. For the first several years of my tenure, I received a weekly printout of every check the seminary cut. Given where we were in our financial life cycle, that was essential. In order to manage cash flow, one has to know what's going out the door in real time. I requested and reviewed the report out of necessity, but it proved beneficial in other ways.

As the months passed, I found myself learning not just what was going out the door but to whom it was going, why it was going there, and who initiated the spend. It was an illuminating process that resulted in significant institutional savings. We found leases to not renew, contracts to renegotiate, and, of course, unnecessary expenses to eliminate.

But, more importantly, it expedited my institutional learning curve. I quickly got my mind around when, where, and how much money was going out the door.

I no longer must track the money check by check, but I still carefully review our monthly financial statements and strategically chart our long-term financial goals. If something goes awry, I may not be the responsible party, but I am the accountable one. More important, faithful stewardship demands such intentionality from my office.

Avoid the Big Two

Most organizations make two big financial mistakes: they build buildings they don't need and hire people they can't afford.

Dedicating new buildings can be exhilarating. In fact, few things excite an institutional community like seeing construction crews on a campus. The ribbon-cutting ceremonies are sweet, memorable occasions. Legacy-minded leaders like to point to buildings completed during their tenure. What is more, the tangibility of the project generally makes the fundraising task more manageable than other, less visible needs.

But there are downsides. Huge downsides. The first is the enormous time associated with planning the project, raising the money, and overseeing the construction project through to completion. Such construction projects have led to the downfall of many leaders.

But the long-term costs are greater still. The building will need to be maintained, heated and cooled, insured, cleaned, staffed, etc. And, by the way, its uncanny how our buildings shape us. As a leader, you may find yourself unintentionally staffing up to the number of offices you have on your campus, as opposed to staffing to meet actual needs and in alignment with actual resources.

Similarly, it's easy to believe you're one big hire away from turning the organization around. For instance, in my context, the norms are all broken. Traditional employment models of personnel costs exceeding 70 percent of the operating budget are altogether unsustainable. Administrative redundancy, tenured faculty positions, and underpopulated degree programs all intensify the challenge.

But that's how the typical institution operates, one might respond. That may be true, but the typical institution is also broke, trapped in an unsustainable business model, and facing financial exigency—whether they realize it or not.

Complicating matters further, a bloated head count leads to chronic underpayment, which limits your ability to recruit and retain the personnel you need. It can be a downward spiral that's difficult to grow out of and painful to cut your way out of. That's why it's best to avoid it altogether.

Lastly, remember buildings and personnel both make for fixed expenses as opposed to discretionary ones. Fixed expenses are harder to curb and nearly impossible to control in absolute terms. The higher your fixed expenses are as a percentage of your operating budget, the lower your discretionary spending will be. What is more, higher fixed costs undermine your ability to build financial margin. And if you're running metal on metal, you're one disappointing business cycle away from catastrophe.

Realize the Power of Compound Interest

Albert Einstein referred to compound interest as the eighth wonder of the world. The way of compound interest is amazing indeed. Most leaders think of compound interest in only personal terms; we must think organizationally as well.

Over the years, I've sought to drill this point home with my kids. At the dinner table I've thrown scenarios at them like: "If right now, at age ten, you started investing $100 per month, and it compounded at 10 percent annually, how much would that be worth at age seventy?" The kids would say something like "$60,000," and be absolutely floored when I said, "Actually, about $4.7 million." That's the power of compound interest, and it will work to your advantage—or your disadvantage.

Compound interest works in both directions. For instance, consider this conversation I recently had with a colleague here at Midwestern Seminary. We were discussing whether to create a position, with a salary of about $75,000 per year. All told, including benefits and support costs, the position would be about a $100,000 a year hit to the budget. Typically, it's a win simply to get the budget manager to factor in the immediate benefit costs.

In trying to explain the budget impact, however, I invited the colleague into my thinking. I reflected:

Let's say God gives me another thirty years of service and that employee serves with me all those years. And assume that between cost-of-living adjustments, merit raises, and escalating benefit costs, their budget impact increases 5 percent per year for thirty years. Do you know what the total seminary outlay will be over that time? Almost $7 million!

Conversely, if the seminary took that $100,000 per year and invested it for thirty years, compounding at 10 percent interest annually, that would total almost $19 million. You read that right—$19 million!

Do you see the math? A new hire isn't just a $75,000 or $100,000 decision. It's not even a $7 million decision. If God enables me to serve another thirty years, it may well be a $26 million decision!

Now of course this logic breaks down at some point. We need people to fulfill the mission entrusted to us. And to fulfill that mission, we create positions and hire new people all the time. Likewise, we've undertaken numerous construction projects and will likely do so in the future. But we should never do so blindly, unaware of the real and potential financial costs. We must enter these with eyes wide open, especially aware of the compounding costs.

Along these lines, there are two extremes to avoid. On the one extreme is hypersensitivity to money. We're a seminary, not a bank or an investment firm. We must remember our enduring mission. On the other extreme, we're not an employment agency or a construction company. The stewardship-minded leader is aware of these financial realities, even when he knowingly makes decisions that push against them.

There are two themes you should detect in this chapter. The first is that every step of the way God has blessed us financially, and that has made all the difference. The second is that carefully stewarding those blessings will make a greater difference.

Covid: An Unexpected Stress Test

For Midwestern Seminary, like most every other organization, COVID-19 presented the ultimate financial stress test. Overnight we faced the high likelihood of shortfalls in every revenue stream. Churches couldn't meet, thus giving was expected to plummet. The stock market cratered, crimping endowment spending and donors' appetite to give. A move to online classes would set back auxiliary revenue streams like housing and meal plans. It all appeared to be the perfect storm.

As I huddled with my senior leadership team, we iterated through various scenarios. We planned on a continuum: one end projected catastrophic shortfalls; the other only mild impacts.

We were determined to come out of COVID stronger than we entered into it, even if that meant making hard decisions. Similar institutions slashed their payrolls, instituted across-the-board salary reductions, and froze benefits. Everything looked bleak. To overreact would cause unnecessary pain to employees and harm to the institution. But to underreact could bring other negative ramifications, financial and otherwise.

And we emerged from it financially stronger, not weaker. That speaks to the resilience of the seminary's team, kind providence in our revenue streams, and our quick adjustments, demonstrating the institutional agility we'd long valued.

COVID-19 was the ultimate stress test for us, as it was for most everyone else. We came through it in a position of strength with minimal institutional disruption, financially speaking. Years of sound stewardship and strategic contingency planning made that possible.

In Conclusion

Three organizational questions dominate my thinking these days, one of which concerns the topic at hand: How do we build an ever-strengthening institution in an ever-weakening context?

Most schools are either plateaued or declining in enrollment, and the financial outlook is bleak for a similar number of institutions. Even the best-led institutions aren't immune from outgoing tides.

And, as a leader, you increasingly realize what control you do and don't have over these factors. You have more influence over the resources you possess than you do over potential resources. In other words, stewarding what you have is more crucial—and more doable—than increasing what you have.

This is important to remember. And take heart, a healthy organization can be financially strengthening even as its weakening in some other area. The wise leader recognizes these realities and works accordingly.

As a boy, I well recall my grandmother's stories about the Great Depression. In a sense, they were so impoverished before it hit that Black Tuesday wasn't much darker for them. But she told stories of extreme need, of true deprivation, of her father leaving the farm for extended periods looking for work. Since she'd seen the Great Depression once, she knew it could happen again. She lived her life and managed her money accordingly.

My early years at Midwestern Seminary were my Great Depression experience. I know what it's like to be flat broke institutionally, to pray for gifts to pay bills, and to hustle across the country on crisis fundraising ventures. Those experiences were life-shaping for me. They remain paradigmatic for my leadership. Learn from my experience, but purpose not to have to live it. Steward your money.

9

Communicate Clearly

I n history's most consequential hours, the tongue has proven more powerful than the sword. At least this is the takeaway from the twentieth century. Two twentieth-century developments made this true: new means of mass destruction and new means of mass communication—and the orators who used it.

When we think of great communicators, we tend to think of political leaders on history's grandest stages rallying their people toward noble, heroic ends. In fact, the twentieth century didn't just create such moments; it necessitated them. For instance, think of President Franklin Roosevelt and his memorable perorations. To a joint session of Congress, he declared: "December 7, 1941, a day that will live in infamy."[1]

Similarly, his insistence on mankind's four freedoms, his rousing call for America to become an arsenal for democracy, and his shepherding the nation through years of economic hardship and world war via his fireside chats are all evidence of the power of communication.

Two decades later, in the hottest hours of the Cold War, John F. Kennedy's inaugural address became a high note of twentieth-century oratory. Brimming with energy and optimism, Kennedy called for freedom's defense and summoned national service. His immortal words still resound over six decades later:

> Let every nation know, whether it wishes us well or ill, that we shall pay any price, bear any burden, meet any hardship, support any friend, oppose any foe to assure the survival and the success of liberty. This much we pledge—and more.
>
> And so, my fellow Americans: ask not what your country can do for you—ask what you can do for your country. My fellow citizens of the world: ask not what America will do for you, but what together we can do for the freedom of man.[2]

Consider Churchill

Of the twentieth century's greatest orators, none stir the spirit like Winston Churchill. In the jaws of Nazi aggression, Churchill rallied his people to withstand Hitler's deathly assault. With Europe ravaged and France fallen, Churchill infused his people with resolve, bucking them up throughout the terrors of the Battle of Britain.

His turn of phrase, colorful life experiences, decades of practice, mastery of the English language, and the crucible of World War II all combined to give Churchill, and his speeches, an almost mythological status.

Consider these excerpts from just a few of his speeches. Imagine the wartime moment in which he spoke. Put yourself in the place of his hearers. Upon receiving His Majesty's commission to form a new government, thus becoming prime minister in his nation's darkest hour, he soberly warned his parliamentary colleagues:

> I would say to the House, as I said to those who have joined this government: "I have nothing to offer but blood, toil, tears and sweat.[3]

For his nation, Churchill described the crisis before them:

We have before us an ordeal of the most grievous kind. We have before us many, many long months of struggle and of suffering. You ask, what is our policy? I can say: It is to wage war, by sea, land and air, with all our might and with all the strength that God can give us; to wage war against a monstrous tyranny, never surpassed in the dark, lamentable catalogue of human crime. That is our policy.

You ask, what is our aim? I can answer in one word: It is victory, victory at all costs, victory in spite of all terror, victory, however long and hard the road may be; for without victory, there is no survival.[4]

Speaking to his nation after the Dunkirk evacuation and before what appeared to be the imminent Nazi invasion of the British Isles, Churchill again rallied his people:

I have, myself, full confidence that if all do their duty, if nothing is neglected, and if the best arrangements are made, as they are being made, we shall prove ourselves once again able to defend our Island home, to ride out the storm of war, and to outlive the menace of tyranny, if necessary for years, if necessary, alone.[5]

Even though large tracts of Europe and many old and famous States have fallen or may fall into the grip of the Gestapo and all the odious apparatus of Nazi rule, we shall not flag or fail.

We shall go on to the end, we shall fight in France, we shall fight on the seas and oceans, we shall fight with growing confidence and growing strength in the air, we shall defend our Island, whatever the cost may be, we shall fight on the beaches, we shall fight on the landing grounds, we shall fight in the fields and in the streets, we shall fight in the hills; we shall never surrender.[6]

Lastly, speaking again with the German invasion apparently imminent, Churchill surveyed the dark horizon and pointed his people upward, to glory.

> What General Weygand called the Battle of France is over. I expect that the Battle of Britain is about to begin. Upon this battle depends the survival of Christian civilization. Upon it depends our own British life, and the long continuity of our institutions and our Empire. The whole fury and might of the enemy must very soon be turned on us. Hitler knows that he will have to break us in this Island or lose the war.
>
> Let us therefore brace ourselves to our duties, and so bear ourselves that, if the British Empire and its Commonwealth last for a thousand years, men will still say, "This was their finest hour."[7]

At these strategic moments, in times of true national crisis, Churchill knew his people needed something more than ships, tanks, and artillery. They needed courage. They needed willpower. And his speeches proved to do what armaments alone could not—defeat Nazi aggression. Indeed, Edward R. Murrow was spot-on when he famously quipped: "Churchill mobilized the English language and sent it into battle."[8]

In this chapter, however, we need more than inspiration from past orators and their glorious speeches. We need to rediscover the necessity of clear communication. And we need to learn how, regardless of your context, to practice it.

You don't have to be Churchill to communicate clearly, but you must learn to do so. For to lead is to communicate, and to lead well is to communicate with excellence.

Multidirectional Communication

For starters, you must understand that leaders communicate in multiple directions. We naturally think of one direction or another, but we must think holistically. You communicate in at least four directions: downward, upward, internally, and externally. This is what I call multidirectional communication.

Downward Communication

To make this point, I'll use myself and Midwestern Seminary as an example. First, I communicate downward to those under me on the organizational chart. This starts with my direct reports but includes speaking through them to their respective areas of oversight. It also includes when I speak directly to their reports, to their entire division, or to our institutional community.

It's not enough to detect the realms of your communication. You must also sense the power of the words you use. This is especially true with downward communication.

Many leaders give insufficient thought to their downward communication. Because someone's on their payroll, they assume that they can take them for granted or communicate however they wish, including harshly.

If this is your pattern, you will not retain your best employees. And those you do retain will simmer with resentment and bitterness, becoming toxic to those around them. That's not how you build a winning team. That's how you destroy one.

Your words have the power to wound or to heal, to tear down or to build up, to inspire or to deflate, to draw in or to push away. It's in your best interest to communicate well with those you lead. For instance, reflect on these phrases and consider how they'll land on the ear—and in the hearts—of those you lead.

- I'm so thankful you're on my team.
- I not only trust you, but I also believe in you.
- I know you can do this. I know you can.
- Feel free to reach out to me for more clarity.
- That's really helpful!
- How can I help you accomplish what I've asked you to do?
- I promise you I will read and reflect on your proposal.
- How is your family?
- How was your weekend?
- How can I better lead you, serve you, support you?
- Here's what success will look like for you.
- How can I pray for you?
- What do you think?
- Please, come in.
- I'm sorry. I apologize. Please forgive me.
- I forgive you. Think nothing more of it.
- Here's how you can best help me.
- Here's how I'd like you to handle that in the future.
- Do you feel like this is clear?
- Let me make sure I understand you.

Do you see how life-giving these phrases can be? And note, most every one of these phrases could've been conveyed in a similar but more deflating way. For instance, "Here's how you can best help me" lands better than, "That wasn't helpful." Or, "Here's how I'd like you to handle that in the future" is better than, "You handled that poorly." And doesn't, "Do you feel like this is clear?" land better than "Am I clear?"

Now, to be honest, I've used both phrases in these couplets. There are times, say, if a team member has acted inappropriately despite prior instruction, when "Am I clear?" is the most appropriate phrase to use. The key is to bring the amount of intensity that the circumstances merit and that you intend. To soft-pedal a serious transgression helps no one; neither does going to DEFCON 1 over a mild offense.

Praise in Public. Praise your employees in public, including those who mean most to them. For instance, I'll often send notes of appreciation to an employee's home address because their family will more likely see my words of praise.

Or, as another example, when meeting an employee's children, I love to brag on the mom or dad who works here. Our workforce is small enough that I know, or at least know of, most every employee. Thus, I can usually speak to them and their family personally. To brag on that employee in front of their family is an absolute delight.

To a child I might say, "Did you know your mother is a very important person here?" The smiles go all the way around. To visiting parents I might say, "Your son is a gifted scholar. He's making a real difference here and is truly impacting the churches we serve. You should be proud of him." I love to see those parents well up with pride in their adult child.

That's Right! Along these lines, consider the phrase "That's right." In his book, *Never Split the Difference: Negotiating as if Your Life Depends on It*, Chris Voss introduces the importance of this phrase. Voss retired as the FBI's senior hostage negotiator. He argues the phrase is key to developing rapport and empathy with your interlocutor, whether it's in a hostage negotiation or inside a boardroom.[9]

If the other person says, "That's right," it means they're tracking with you and believe you understand their point of view. In other words, if the other person nods his head and mutters, "That's right," it means you're on the right track.[10]

I've learned to listen for such phrases as I dialogue with my team members. They're dutiful enough to run the plays I give them, but if I want real buy-in—and a real, long-term emotional connection with them—I need to involve them in my thinking and make sure they know that I understand theirs.

Finally, communicate to your subordinates how you expect them to communicate to you. Let them know the reports you desire, the timeliness associated with them, and the data they should contain.

By way of personal illustration, my team knows I don't want to learn from social media that they're hiking the Appalachian Trail. They also know I prefer to be overcommunicated with, thus, I value simple FYI emails.

Upward Communication

Conversely, though I'm the seminary's president, I too communicate upwardly. I report to our board of trustees. Communicating with those to whom you report takes intentionality. Every overseer has different expectations.

I probably err in communicating too much, not too little. Candidly, it can be a difficult balance. Communicating too much may seem like a data dump. Communicating too little insufficiently honors their role as overseers. My operating principle is, "If I were a trustee, what would I want to know? And, as president, what do I need to ensure they know?"

The challenging part of the work is that organizations, including theological institutions, are dynamic places. They're not static. Trustees come and go (as do employees), so you will sound repetitive to some while conveying entirely new information to others. Work to provide the essential facts and strive never to surprise them.

For your upward reports, including your board of trustees, remember this: they want good news; they know they'll occasionally hear bad. But they will not tolerate false news, and they shouldn't. Give them the facts, unvarnished. That one thing you most want not to tell your boss is what you should most urgently tell them.

I've repeatedly told my team that I *want* to hear good news promptly but that I *demand* to hear bad news promptly. There's a human tendency to bury bad news, hoping to right the situation alone and, thus, avoid having to pass along bad news.

Parents are all too familiar with the example I use to make this point. Imagine a child who is getting low marks in math class. Fear of disappointment or punishment prompts them to conceal the struggle, with the news coming out after the low grades are baked into the semester transcript. If they'd notified the parent earlier, there would've been time to correct the situation. A timely parent-teacher conference or the aid of a tutor may have led to a course correction.

My team knows to get me disappointing news immediately. If they notify me far enough upstream, we may be able to remedy the situation, making it relatively painless. Delaying bad news almost always makes it worse, not better.

All of this is to say, words matter, especially when communicating to those who report to you. But they also matter when you're communicating with your superiors. For example, consider these phrases and how they'll land on your boss's ears.

- What would it look like for me to exceed your expectations?
- How can I better serve you?
- Am I getting you everything you need from me?
- When would you like me to get back with you?
- How can I best honor you in this?
- Am I communicating with you well enough?
- Is there anything I can take off your plate today?
- I sense this is important to you. Don't worry; I won't drop the ball.
- Rest easy. You can count on me.

Lastly, remember your boss is your boss. He's not your spouse. His antennae can only be so active. Don't hope he'll pick up on your subtle signals. If something is on your mind, express it and do so clearly. If a message needs to be conveyed, state it. Don't insinuate it.

And whatever you do, start with the bottom line and work backwards. If your boss needs more content, he'll ask you to elaborate. Don't take him on a conversational journey, meandering through a narrative that may mean something to you but is unhelpful to him. That's the quickest way to make your boss dread his meetings with you.

Internal Communication

The most important factor in internal communication is to know, contextually, what your organization faces and where you are in your leadership life cycle. These changing dynamics matter immensely.

For instance, when you're new to the organization, it's virtually impossible to overcommunicate. As Hans Finzel states, "There is never a time when more inhouse communication is needed than when a new leader arrives on the scene. People need to know what to expect of their new leader. If you are that person, make sure you overcommunicate as an obsession."[11]

Or consider how organizations, like Midwestern Seminary, change. For example, ten years ago Midwestern Seminary had about one thousand students, most of whom were distance-education students. We had dozens of employees, not hundreds. All-staff meetings could be held in a relatively small room. The community was tight, and that made communication easier.

As I write this chapter, we are now an institution of some five thousand students and a few hundred employees. As a senior faculty member recently remarked, "Mr. President, we now have more employees than we did students when I first came to teach here."

Again, Finzel helps us on this point, writing, "As organizations grow from small entrepreneurships into professionally managed organizations, communication must be given more attention and must become more formal.... The bigger the group, the more attention must be given to communication."[12]

For example, during my early years the community was small enough, and we were in close enough proximity, that we could make communication simple. I could insinuate, drop hints, and send signals with the assurance that our employees would catch my drift. The circumstances made direct, awkward words of instruction less necessary.

We passed that as a workable form of communication years ago. The size of the institution and the dispersion of our community mean that I must communicate with clarity, eliminating the margin for error. That means, at times, I'm more direct or forceful than I'd prefer, but the margin of error is small enough that I have no other option.

For instance, consider the world of politics. A candidate's biggest fear is not his opponent doing something brilliant; his biggest fear is one of his staffers doing or saying something foolish. That translates, at least to some degree, to most every organizational setting. In my world, one errant tweet can cause significant disruption.

Along these lines, I've found direct, clarifying conversations can be awkward but more pleasant than a corrective one. And a timely, strategic word of clarification often makes corrective conversations unnecessary.

One final word on this front. A few times circumstances have necessitated I bring the heat in altogether unpleasant ways. On those occasions, to do so was an act of love, though it might not have felt like it at the time. Sometimes the most loving thing you can do is to dress someone down. On balance, I think I've erred in having too few of those conversations, not too many.

In summary, a lack of internal communication leads to confusion, which often leads to speculation, gossip, and a host of other ailments for your organization. Always err on the side of overcommunication.

External Communication

As to the last direction, consider external communication. We'll be brief on this point because you're most likely already convinced of its importance. Communicating externally, to your constituency, is near the top of the organizational leader's to-do list.

In the corporate world, we usually equate external communication with one's customers. While it's appropriate for businesses to do this, in my context external communication is about projecting to students and churches our identity, convictions, and mission and how we equip students in light of those.

In addition to communicating our beliefs and our mission, I'm also, at one level or another, saying, "Here are our needs; support us. Here are our victories; celebrate with us. Here are our opportunities; help us. Here are our goals; root for us. Here is our mission; join us."

Choose Your Medium of Communication Wisely

How you communicate is nearly as important as what you communicate. Ask yourself: *What am I trying to communicate? Is this a brief word of update? A clear word of direction? The announcement of a major new initiative? Is this a word of caution? Or a cause for celebration?* What you're trying to say will shape how you say it.

In general, the more time the message takes to deliver, the more personal and more meaningful it will be. For example, consider the messaging waterfall: in-person, Zoom, phone call, handwritten note, email, text, social media post. Do you see the correlation? The more time it takes, the more meaningful it will be.

If you have a serious message, don't communicate it in an unserious format. If you have an urgent message, don't send it via snail mail. If you're passing along a word of update, email will suffice. If you're trying to touch a heart, work to visit in person.

As a final example, consider the COVID-19 pandemic. Crisis communication, such as COVID-19 mandated, usually requires three things: clarity, brevity, and frequency. The more frequently you sense you'll need to communicate, the briefer you'll be. Timeliness will be more important than thoroughness, especially if the crisis is evolving.

Pronouncing the Word No

Lastly, I remind you that the most essential word in the leader's vocabulary is *no*. And pronouncing that word is one of the leader's most important responsibilities.

Saying "no" did not come naturally to me. I could spit it out when pushed, but I preferred to steer clear of it. I was equipped to say no over issues of doctrine, conviction, and morality. But I was much less capable of saying "no" over more subjective, less consequential issues, especially when asked by someone I knew and liked.

I look back on earlier years and see responsibilities and requests I granted because I wasn't comfortable pronouncing that simple, two-letter, one-syllable word. Those exchanges went something like this:

- Can we make this presentation in church? Um, Okay.
- Would you and your family please attend our party? Sure.
- Do you mind if we start this new ministry initiative? That's fine.
- Will you counsel our (nonchurch member) grandson? I guess I can.
- Will you speak at our event? Would love to.

In hindsight, I didn't go along out of fear of conflict. I was reticent to disappoint. I was just reluctant to let someone down. The result usually wasn't disaster, but it often diluted my energies and resources. And, of course, it was poor stewardship of my time.

Additionally, saying "yes" often curtailed my ability to give time and energy to other more worthy causes, including church and family. The adage is true; when you say "yes" to one thing, you are saying "no" to another.

These are small examples, but learning to say "no" in small things makes saying "no" in the big things easier. The higher the stakes, the greater the pressure to acquiesce will be. That's why, for me, learning to pronounce the word *no* was both liberating and confidence-instilling.

Again, Look to Churchill

I'll never forget the moment it first began to sink in that I had to learn to pronounce the word *no*. I was listening to a speech by Winston Churchill, and in it he admonished the free world to do the same.

Summoning the wisdom of Alexander the Great, Churchill called upon the free world to muster the courage to tell Hitler no. In his famous October 16, 1938, broadcast to the United States and England named "The Defence of Freedom and Peace (The Lights Are Going Out)," Churchill reflected:

> Alexander the Great remarked that the people of Asia were slaves because they had not learned to pronounce the word "No." Let that not be the epitaph of the English-speaking peoples or of Parliamentary democracy, or of France, or of the many surviving liberal States of Europe.[13]

Regardless of whether one is leading a nation, a seminary, a church, a family, or any other earthly entity, every proposal cannot be met with affirmation. The word *no* may be the most indispensable word in a leader's lexicon.

Whether it is to decline an unsound proposal, scuttle an ill-advised initiative, or just pass up a good idea to pursue a better one, you must learn to pronounce the word *no*.

In Conclusion

Where you are in your relationship context will determine how and what you communicate. Is this a new team member who needs to be instructed or a tenured, apparently insubordinate employee who needs to be reprimanded? Is this an aggressive employee who needs to be reined in or a beleaguered employee who needs to be motivated?

And whatever you do, continue to communicate the mission and the vision. Remember, vision leaks. You simply can't overcommunicate it. And as you do, you'll be a leader, not just a manager. As Churchill said, "The difference between mere management and leadership is communication." That's why you must communicate clearly.

10

Foster the Right Culture

Peter Drucker famously argued that "culture eats strategy for breakfast." I've found every syllable of Drucker's maxim to be true. It's been true of every organization I've served or closely observed. And it's certainly been true for Midwestern Seminary. Culture matters—far more than you may think.

Think of an organization's culture as its feel, its vibe, its spirit, its personality. An organization's culture tends to be a cocktail, a mixture of its values, standards, personalities, and ambitions.

An organization's culture comes together like your grandmother's best recipe: two scoops of this, a pinch of that, a dash of something else, and a mysterious smidgen of one last ingredient thrown on top. Why settle for precise measurements when her imprecise ones come together oh-so well? Measured precision might just ruin it all.

The same is true of healthy cultures. An organization's culture is more detected than documented, more overheard than heard, more sensed than seen. If an organization's culture is healthy, you'll likely know it. If it's unhealthy, you definitely will.

More formally, Hanz Finzel notes: "An organization's corporate culture is the way insiders behave based on the values and group traditions they hold."[1]

With a bit more elaboration, Ralph Kilmann argues:

The organization itself has an invisible quality—a certain style, a character, a way of doing things—that may be more powerful than the dictates of any one person or any formally documented system. To understand the essence or soul of the organization requires that we travel below the charts, rulebooks, machines, and buildings into the underground world of corporate cultures.[2]

I can't think of organizational culture without thinking of Steve Jobs. At Apple, Jobs was a culture hawk. In Walter Isaacson's award-wining biography of Jobs, he recounted how obsessed Apple's leader was with culture. Jobs believed culture was not only essential to Apple's success in the near-term, but essential to its future success for generations to come.

Jobs studied leading corporations like Ford Motor Company that had stood the test of time. He reflected on what gave them enduring relevance and intergenerational success. Why did Ford endure and not, say, Studebaker, or other automobile manufacturers that have long since gone belly-up?

Jobs concluded it went back to its organizational culture—that collection of beliefs, priorities, standards, and practices that made such companies unique and endurable. Jobs worked to encode such cultural distinctives within Apple's DNA.

He believed the more deeply these distinctives were embedded in Apple's DNA, the stronger the company would be, and the more resilient and enduring it would prove in the long run. Jobs believed Apple's dominance could endure for decades. So far he has been right.

The Irony of Culture

The stubborn thing about a healthy culture is you can't fake it, nor can you force it. You can't require cheerfulness, nor can you coerce unity. No memo from the CEO's office mandating attitudes and outlooks will work. The CEO can foster culture by what he models, but he can't force it by what he mandates.

Yes, you can create the circumstances for a healthy culture, but even that won't guarantee it. You can't even buy yourself a healthy culture, regardless of how lavishly you spend.

Though a healthy culture can't be prescribed, the attentive leader still strives for it. Just because it's elusive doesn't mean you shouldn't pursue it. In fact, you must pursue it. Even the most obtuse leader knows its value. And even the most tone-deaf listener knows when he doesn't hear its sound.

Yes, there's an irony with organizational culture. There's an inverse correlation between how important it is and one's ability to orchestrate it. If you have a building need, you find the money for the construction costs. If you have a talent need, you look for a strategic hire. If you have a financial need, you look for additional sources of revenue. These scenarios are all formulaic.

In fact, a large part of an organization's work can be orchestrated, but culture can't be. Culture is more of a by-product than a product. It's more of the sweet aroma that emanates from a sumptuous meal than the meal itself.

And, for heaven's sake, don't try to coerce it. Have you ever tried to make your children smile for a family photograph? When our five children were young, family photos were always an adventure. It took magic to get all five children to look at the camera and to smile simultaneously. There was always one—or more than one—child who had a reason to frown. In exasperation, I'd threaten them to smile . . . or else.

For family photos, I suppose forced smiles are better than no smiles, but the best smiles are authentic and reflexive. So it is with organizational culture. The best culture is authentic and reflexive, emanating from satisfied, cheerful, on-mission team members. Those heart postures, taken together, make for a cheerful, dynamic organizational culture. I wouldn't try to coerce it even if I thought I could; it would do more harm than good.

Consider Midwestern Seminary

Midwestern Seminary's culture has been a key ingredient to our success. And we've gotten much more out of it than we've put into it.

Like the United States Marine Corps, we want our own *esprit de corps*, one that is distinct to Midwestern. Emulate us if you want; that's flattering. But don't think for one minute you can bottle up our culture. If it could be bottled up, we'd have done so and sold it long ago. Culture doesn't work that way.

We want to be convictional, cheerful, and institutionally confident. We aspire to be humble, sincere, and gracious. We emphasize maximum effort to achieve our goals and thankfulness when we do. We understand we are a fallen people, so we aspire to be redemptive with one another. Forgiveness isn't subject to supply shortages with God; it ought not be so with us either.

And, of course, we are *for the church*. Before making a hire, we ask ourselves: *Are they for the church? Do they so resonate with our mission that it really is their mission too? Are they going to enhance our for-the-church commitment? Will they enhance our for-the-church culture?*

Investor Warren Buffett suggests companies should build a moat around their enterprise, a protective area that prevents the competition from overtaking your castle of success. If Midwestern Seminary has a moat, it would have to be our culture.

But for us, it's better than a moat. It's essential to our secret sauce.

Culture, Essential to Organizational Momentum

A healthy culture is essential to your organization's momentum. Momentum propels an organization forward. Wins are more attainable and goals are more achievable. For us, a culture of joy, mission-focus, attainable goals, and extreme ownership all feed our momentum.

Milton Friedman, one of the twentieth century's leading economists, famously illustrated how one small, seemingly insignificant factor can stall a major economy. Friedman used an automobile to make his point. He said you can have a $30,000 car with everything working perfectly, but it can be immobilized by a dead $30 battery. The battery cost .1 percent of the automobile, but it can shut down the car entirely.

That's the way culture works. It's so small it's organizationally undetectable. Yet if it isn't right, it will be an unseeable—but insurmountable—headwind. It will stall forward momentum.

Interestingly, culture doesn't occupy a building on campus. It doesn't have an office staff for support. It doesn't have its own stationary, nor does it show up in strategic-planning sessions. You won't see culture on campus wayfinding. And financially speaking, culture is budgetarily indetectable. It costs you nothing, but a lack of it will cost you everything.

An institution can have spectacular facilities, an accomplished faculty, a large endowment, and other obvious strengths, but if it lacks a healthy culture, it won't hit its full potential. If it has a bad culture, it'll noticeably underperform. If an institution permits a toxic culture, it'll soon find itself in a state of crisis.

And all of this will go back to something that seems so small.

Alan Kohll calls culture "the backbone of a happy workforce." Note the upside of a healthy culture, as he continues:

> There's a reason why companies who are named as a *Best Place to Work* see so much success. These organizations tend to have strong, positive corporate cultures that help employees feel

and perform their best at work. Research gathered by Culture IQ found that employees' overall ratings of their company's qualities—including collaboration, environment and values—are rated 20% higher at companies that exhibit strong culture.[3]

Patrick Lencioni argues that "the single greatest advantage any company can achieve is organizational health. Yet it is ignored by most leaders even though it is simple, free, and available to anyone who wants it."[4] Lencioni continues: "I've become absolutely convinced that the seminal difference between successful companies and mediocre or unsuccessful ones has little, if anything, to do with what they know or how smart they are; it has everything to do with how healthy they are."[5]

Healthy culture is essential to your organization; thus, it's essential to your leadership. Learn to recognize it when you see it, to be concerned when you don't, and to foster it along the way.

The High Costs of Bad Culture

The costs of a bad culture are too high to pay. You can't afford it. What you'll lose in time, momentum, joy, and effectiveness is incalculable. In fact, organizational theorists often cite, literally, the high costs of a bad culture. Along these lines, Patrick Lencioni argues:

> The financial cost of having an unhealthy organization is undeniable: wasted resources and time, decreased productivity, increased employee turnover, and customer attrition. The money an organization loses as a result of these problems, and the money it has to spend to recover them, is staggering.[6]

And note, there are more ways to lose than just by permitting a toxic culture. Yes, that would be ruinous. But a bland, indistinctive culture will also saddle your organization. Instead, cultivate organizational distinctives that represent your mission and enhance your community.

Building a Healthy Culture, Consider Midwestern Seminary

God has blessed us with a fantastic culture at Midwestern Seminary. To be sure, we're far from perfect. But we value candidness, keep short accounts, and aggressively root out passive-aggressive behavior. Though the precise wording varies, I'm consistently struck by how often people describe us as happy, joyous, winsome, or cheerful.

The common thread is that visitors detect a cheerfulness that's often lacking in institutional settings. And, given the challenging circumstances most institutions abide in, that's not surprising. What is surprising is how, in the main, our campus community is cheerful. In fact, people often refer to us as the happy seminary. That's one reason our employee turnover rate tends to be low while our list of candidates for job openings is typically high.

In fact, this became clear a few years back during an accreditation review session. In contrast to my first accreditation encounter, this one was altogether different. While on campus, this accreditation site-visit team interviewed several faculty and staff. Their reflections on the institution were so positive that the interviewing accreditors suggested we'd stocked the pool with preselected employees and had coached them in how to answer the questions!

Of course, nothing could have been further from the truth. But that entire episode did remind me how unique a healthy culture is and that I shouldn't take it for granted. Neither should you in your own context.

As I've argued from the beginning of this chapter, you can't choreograph a healthy culture, but you can foster it. You can't ensure it, but you can cultivate it.

The culture of Midwestern Seminary is always on my mind. I don't mean I'm always tinkering with it, turning knobs this way or that. No, but I'm constantly aware of it because it recurringly shows up in my life. When I talk with employees, I sense it. When I visit with students, I hear it. When I bump into campus visitors, they comment on it.

For just one example, consider a recurring conversation I enjoy. I routinely ask students, "Who's your favorite professor?" typically followed with "Why?" It's uncanny how often the answers, one way or another, go back to that professor's embodiment of the seminary's culture.

On occasion a student will answer, "Because he wrote two books last year," but usually the response is less tangible, less quantifiable. More commonly I get answers like, "She's always willing to help me," "He goes the extra mile with his students," "She's always cheerful, happy to see me," or "I love how devoted he is to the local church."

Do you see what's happening in those conversations? Though the students don't even realize it, their answers reflect subjective, cultural aspects of our institutional identity, as embodied in the individual professors.

Four Keys to Fostering a Healthy Culture

As I've argued, a healthy culture isn't formulaic. You can't mandate it, nor can you ensure it. But you can foster it. Over the years I've found these four keys to be instrumental in our culture. You won't find them emblazoned on a wall somewhere (though perhaps you should). They are, however, often on our minds and lips.

First, *hire the right people*. In Washington, D.C., they say that personnel is policy. That is, who you hire will determine the policies that are pursued. In higher education, they say that the faculty is the curriculum. The faculty you hire determines what will be taught. When it comes to your organization, people are the culture.

If you hire toxic people, you'll have a toxic culture. If you hire cynics, you'll see cynicism in your ranks. If you hire negative people, negativity will show up. Conversely, if you hire sanguine, sunny people, you'll be pleasantly surprised at how rarely the organizational forecast is cloudy.

Look for people who not only resonate with your organization, but whom you can see embodying it. You want employees who don't just agree with your mission, but who personify it. Look for employees who not only appreciate your culture, but who will strengthen it.

And on this front, one's track record matters. Anyone can have a bad employment experience, but if someone's résumé is littered with them, they're likely the problem, not their previous places of service. As they say, if you run into a jerk in the morning, you ran into a jerk. If you run into jerks all day, you're the jerk.

If you want a cheerful culture, don't hire people who are always seething. If you want an ambitious culture, don't hire people who are lazy. If you want a godly culture, don't hire people marked by carnality.

There's more to a healthy culture than hiring the right people, but there's not less to it. A healthy culture starts by hiring the right people. So do just that.

And, by the way, there's a self-fulfilling, reinforcing cycle on this point. Personnel who embody a healthy culture enable you to recruit and retain others who do the same.

Second, *hold high the right principles*. By right principles, I mean your organization's convictions, mission, and vision. Additionally, you should hold high your core values, whether they're formally adopted or informally conveyed. You must continually point your people upward and onward.

As Prasanna Singaraju reminds us:

> You will be surprised how many employees are not aware of their organization's vision, mission and values. It is a very common scenario, and I have seen it happen far too many times. Please take the extra step to effectively communicate the core tenets of your organization—vision, mission and values—to your employees. That can help them to stay more active, aware and motivated. Also, remember to do this every time you have an opportunity to connect with a larger set of people. It's OK to overcommunicate.[7]

You'll also do well to give your team the *why*. Give them the *why* of their service. Tell them why the beliefs, mission, and vision all matter. Tell them why their work is noble, essential, and much bigger than themselves. Show them how their work impacts others for good and why their service and attitude are essential to organizational health.

Also, give them the why when it comes to major decisions, whether specific to you or to the organization. People love hearing the why from the leader. It gives them a sense of ownership. Pragmatically, it makes them more inclined to support decisions that come from the top. You honor your team by giving them the why. They'll most likely honor you and your decisions if you do.

And this, too, is key to organizational health, as it helps fill in the organizational narrative and thus foster greater unity and camaraderie. As Lencioni writes:, "At its core, organizational health is about integrity, but not in the ethical or moral way that integrity is defined so often today. An organization has integrity—is healthy—when it is whole, consistent, and complete, that is, when its management, operations, strategy, and culture fit together and make sense."[8]

At the more granular level, as a seminary we value cheerful conviction and contextual excellence—doing our best with the resources we have. We use words like: *hungry, humble, hustle, excellence, cheerfulness, conviction*, and *stewardship*.

Third, *set the right priorities*. Here, we're intentionally moving one step down from principles. We're moving from the strategic to the tactical.

Many organizations summarize these priorities in their core values. Core values are identified virtues, attitudes, or practices an entity values above all others. They're like road signs or geographical markers to which leaders point to remind stakeholders what matters most.

These priorities are in and of themselves culture markers and culture makers. At Midwestern Seminary we insist on things like extreme ownership. That brings out the best in people, helps them raise their game, and enforces a standard of excellence campus-wide.

We prioritize community and togetherness. Thus, we provide contexts for community and incentivize togetherness. We also value individual responsibility. We talk of remaining institutionally hungry, and we value organizational hustle.

We value personal humility and institutional confidence. We believe God has made us a first-class institution, and we're not afraid to act like it. But since that's a gift from God, it should instill humility not swagger, confidence not arrogance.

Fourth, *establish the right practices.* Lastly, all of this stays theoretical if our daily practices don't enhance culture. So consider just a few of our habits. From generous compensation to timely congratulations, we incentivize the right behavior patterns and institutional outcomes. At the same time, we work to disincentivize the wrong behavior patterns and institutional outcomes.

We routinely invest in team-building. I don't mean we rent out ropes courses and the like. Rather, we plan events, allocate resources, and provide space for togetherness. Midwestern is blessed to have great people working here. Thus, all we have to do is get them together and get out of the way.

We prefer in-person meetings over virtual ones. Yes, there's a place for Zoom, but we're a covenant community, not a loose collection of contract workers. We aren't big on remote work, providing for it only in unique circumstances.

We let people leave. If their hearts have moved beyond the seminary, it's probably best they do too. Those transitions are typically healthy, even sweet. We find joy in commissioning our people unto new places of service.

We aggressively root out passive-aggressive behavior. I'm convinced few deficiencies hinder a leader more than an inability or unwillingness to confront and restore. That's poor leadership, and it ruins organizational culture.

Most important, we are a community of grace. That starts at the top. Our employees know I'm not a grudge-holder, nor do I have a passive-aggressive bone in my body. Employees aren't capriciously consigned to a penalty box somewhere in the back of my mind, stuck there for years without even knowing it.

Philip Eaton well states what we are after in this regard:

> Scriptures are clear and emphatic about the call to build communities of grace. We enter those communities with the commitment to be transformed by the renewing of our minds. We pledge that we will develop the habits of the heart that bring us together in love, grace, kindness, and hospitality. This is our modeling for the world about the real way for organizations to operate effectively. As we align the vision of our organizations to the big idea that the gospel of Jesus Christ holds the power to change the world, we understand then that only through communities of grace will our vision be accomplished.[9]

These *Ps*—people, principles, priorities, and practices—coalesce into what I refer to as the Midwestern Way. Collectively, they contribute to our distinct culture. Without them we'd be adrift and organizationally the weaker for it.

In Conclusion

In recent months I was again reminded of the high value of a healthy institutional culture. I led a strategic retreat with about forty of our senior team members as a post-Covid institutional reset. We prayed together and we played together. We featured key presentations and enjoyed sumptuous meals. It was a rich three days.

The cultural components were more on the back of my mind than the front, but, in hindsight, the big win may have been leaving with a strengthened, healthier culture. And that's just what we needed after sixteen months of face masks, social distancing, and limited togetherness.

Through all of that I learned that just as vision leaks, so does culture. You must steward it, invest in it, and rekindle it. I also learned that a healthy culture surprises to the upside. Stay with me.

We recently announced the addition of a leading scholar to our faculty. The professor is something of a friend, and he's been on our campus and around our faculty on numerous occasions. For some two decades he's taught at a major university, and for most of his time there he's occupied a major endowed chair. He's accomplished in all the right ways—well published, well respected, and well sought after. The list of institutions that have tried to hire him is long, and for many years we were on that list.

Yet in recent months he elected to join us here in Kansas City. It was a major hire, the kind that rippled well beyond the shorelines of theological education.

In conversing with him, I learned that our culture was a decisive factor in his move. I invited him to join us on our faculty retreat as a guest speaker. In so doing, he became more immersed in our team and, thus, in our culture, and found it all increasingly attractive.

Though he occupied a well-funded, prestigious endowed chair at a well-funded, prestigious university, he left all of that to join us. In visiting with him and his spouse about that decision, it became clear our culture was a decisive factor.

And that reminded me anew of how much a healthy culture matters. You can't contrive it, but you must cultivate it. You can't fabricate it, but you must foster it. In short, you must foster the right culture.

CONCLUSION

Like you, I watched with horror as the Notre-Dame Cathedral raged with flames. Not since 9/11 had I sat so transfixed before the television screen, arrested as the unforgiving flames engulfed the storied cathedral. I sat mesmerized as the roof burned, the spire blazed, and the entire edifice itself was humbled before the watching world, bowed low and on the brink of collapse.

Yet I felt a touch of consolation while I watched in disbelief. The previous year my wife and I and our two oldest daughters had visited the iconic structure. We were privileged to tour what appeared to be forever lost.

Everyone who visits the City of Lights has Notre-Dame high on their must-see list. For a seminary president like me, its religious and cultural importance places it at the top. That's why, on that hot July day, I was a man on a mission.

Determined to make the most of our visit, we elbowed our way through Notre-Dame's thirty thousand daily tourists. We saw every sight, heard every presentation, and took in every aspect of Notre-Dame's history and beauty.

You would've done the same. We gazed at the centuries-old organ, were amazed by the cathedral's acoustics, and traced the architectural lines throughout the building, all of which ran vertically, directing our eyes upward.

A Millennium in the Making

Perhaps you recall the story of Notre-Dame. Commissioned by King Louis VII, construction began in 1163 but was not completed until 1345—nearly two centuries later. But to call it completed might be an overstatement. Throughout the centuries, Notre-Dame experienced extended seasons of neglect and damage, and it underwent numerous additions and restorations. Like the people of France, Notre-Dame evolved throughout the second millennium AD.[1]

Among Notre-Dame's architectural distinctions are its pointed arches reaching 108 feet from floor to ceiling. Its crisscrossing, ribbed vaults draw the eyes heavenward, prompting the visitor to contemplate our transcendent God. And most recognizable of all are its flying buttresses, which we'll return to in just a moment.[2]

Notre-Dame is to the French what Westminster Abbey is to the British. It's not just a house of worship; it's a symbol of national history—and the stage for much of it. There in 1431 Henry VI of England was crowned king of France. Napoleon Bonaparte was crowned emperor there in 1804, and a century later Pope Pius X beatified Joan of Arc there.

The site also serves as something of a national vault, housing countless artifacts, treasures, and believed-to-be religious relics, including Jesus's crown of thorns. It's no wonder thirteen million people make the pilgrimage to Notre-Dame each year.

The famed cathedral is a cultural center, an *enduring* source of national pride. Notre-Dame has survived the Protestant Reformation, the French Revolution, the Napoleonic wars, and two world wars. Like time, Notre-Dame marches on.

This storied history is why we all sat transfixed to our screens on April 15, 2019. We beheld so much more than a burning building. We saw a near-millennium's worth of history, heritage, and pride going up in smoke.

At a deeper level, the burning seemed symbolic of a country and a system grown tired, wearied from the weight of history and hollowed out by the secular French state. Indeed, Notre-Dame stood more as a religious mausoleum than a vibrant place of worship for the gathering faithful.

Nonetheless, we looked on in agony as something that took centuries to build was slipping away in minutes. As I watched, my mind returned to our recent visit. I was glad we had beheld Notre-Dame's grandeur, but that experience amplified the sense of loss we all experienced.

The Flying Buttresses

Notre-Dame's flying buttresses stand out to all who have seen the cathedral. Flying buttresses were an architectural innovation of the twelfth century. Typically, interior pillars or exterior walls furnish a building's primary structural support, but flying buttresses, connected to the exterior walls at the roofline, provide support from outside the building.

Flying buttresses proved essential for Notre-Dame's beauty. They enabled the exterior walls to bear less structural support so they could, therefore, feature expansive stained glass and other aesthetic features.

Many architectural historians believe that flying buttresses, a recurring feature of High Gothic architecture, first appeared—at least on a large scale—at Notre-Dame. They were invented to support the Gothic cathedral and to enhance its beauty.

Yes, the flying buttresses are *beautiful*, but they are also *essential*—and they are *obvious*. Without these impossible-to-miss buttresses, the cathedral would not stand. All of this provides a metaphor for leadership, a picture to frame this book and the leadership principles we have explored together.

Obvious, Essential, and Beautiful

Just as the flying buttresses are obvious, essential, and beautiful, so are the ten leadership principles we've considered in this book. And those three descriptors—obvious, essential, and beautiful—aren't accidental. Stay with me.

The flying buttresses are obvious to all who have stood before Notre-Dame. You do not need a trained architectural eye to detect them—you simply need eyes. You might not know their formal, architectural designation, but to be at Notre-Dame is to behold the flying buttresses.

Similarly, the flying buttresses are essential. They're not an aesthetic afterthought but rather an essential, load-bearing feature of the building's architecture. Notre-Dame would not have stood for one thousand years without them, and it might not have survived the fire of 2019. They are essential.

And the flying buttresses are beautiful. They are beautiful in and of themselves, but their load-bearing role also enables and enhances a greater beauty—the beauty that is Notre-Dame.

So it is with the leadership lessons in this book. These ten principles are obvious, essential, and beautiful. They are each, in isolation, beautiful, but they are also resplendent in their collective beauty as to what they foster, create, and project. As you've read this book, I trust you've sensed just that.

And like Notre-Dame's flying buttresses, I am confident these principles are obvious and essential for you, but I am hopeful for more. I hope you will rediscover and apply these principles in ways that make your leadership and the organization you serve into something truly beautiful.

You now know what to do. You now know you can do it. Now, for love of God and neighbor, go do it. Go live and lead up to your own personal and organizational potential. And in so doing, be prepared to create your own turnaround story—a story that's yours for the making!

NOTES

Introduction

1. Winston Churchill, "The Few," International Churchill Society, speech delivered at the House of Commons, London, England, August 20, 1940, https://winstonchurchill.org/resources/speeches/1940-the-finest -hour/the-few.

Chapter 1: Know Your Context

1. "Midwestern at a Glance," Midwestern Baptist Theological Seminary, https://www.mbts.edu/about/#stats.

2. The Commission on Accrediting, The Association of Theological Schools, https://www.ats.edu/uploads/resources/institutional-data/annual-data-tables/2020-2021%20Annual%20Data%20Tables.pdf.

3. Peter Drucker, *The Effective Executive: The Definitive Guide to Getting the Right Things Done* (New York, NY: Harper Business, 2006), 72.

4. John Calvin, *Institutes of the Christian Religion*, vol. I, trans. Henry Beveridge (Carol Stream, IL: Tyndale House, 2008), 1.

5. D. Michael Lindsay, PhD and M. G. Hager, *View from the Top: An Inside Look at How People in Power See and Shape the World* (Hoboken, NJ: John Wiley and Sons, 2014), 64.

6. Drucker, *The Effective Executive*, 96–97.

Chapter 2: Hold Your Convictions

1. Thomas Carlyle, *Sartor Restartus*, ed. Archibald MacMechan (Boston: Athenaeum Press, 1902), 177.

2. R. Albert Mohler, *The Conviction to Lead: 25 Principles for Leadership That Matters* (Minneapolis, MN: Bethany House, 2012), 22.

3. George F. Will, "Biden Exhibits Trumanesque China Policy," *Kansas City Star*, March 28, 2021.

Chapter 3: Define Your Mission

1. This line was said in a speech of thanks given at the House of Commons on Churchill's eightieth birthday on November 30, 1954. See Geoffrey Best, *Churchill: A Study in Greatness* (Oxford: Oxford University Press, 2003), 183.

2. This article has been slightly condensed for space purposes.

3. "Why Is a Company Mission Statement Important?," *Indeed*, February 22, 2021, https://www.indeed.com/career-advice/career-development/why-mission-statement-is-important.

4. "Why Is a Company Mission Statement Important?," *Indeed*, https://www.indeed.com/career-advice/career-development/why-mission-statement-is-important.

5. "Creating a Mission Statement," MRA, https://www.mranet.org/resource/creating-mission-statement.

6. "Mission Statements Are Key to Corporate Strategy Process," AchieveIt, https://www.achieveit.com/resources/blog/mission-statements-key-corporate-strategy-process.

7. David E. Sumner, "What Makes Seminaries Grow?," *In Trust*, Summer 2021, https://intrust.org/Magazine/Issues/Summer-2021/What-makes-seminaries-grow.

Chapter 4: Pursue the Vision

1. "The Commission of Accrediting," The Association of Theological Schools, https://www.ats.edu.

2. Burton Nanus, *Visionary Leadership* (San Franscisco: Jossey-Bass, 1992), 1.

3. United States National Archives and Records Administration, United States Office of the Federal Register, *Weekly Compilation of Presidential Documents* (Washington, D.C.: Office of the Federal Register, National Archives and Records Service, General Services Administration, 1990), 1813.

4. J. Oswald Sanders, *Spiritual Leadership: Principles of Excellence for Every Believer*, updated ed. (Chicago, IL: Moody, 2007), 56.

5. Sanders, *Spiritual Leadership*, 57.

6. Sanders, *Spiritual Leadership*, 58.

7. Bob R. Agee, "Leadership, Vision, and Strategic Planning," in David S. Dockery, ed., *Christian Leadership Essentials: A Handbook for Managing Christian Organizations* (Nashville, TN: B&H Academic, 2011), 50.

8. "22 Vision Statement Examples to Help You Write Your Own," Brex, September 8, 2021, https://www.brex.com/blog/vision-statement-examples.

9. Jonathan Parnell, "Leader, Articulate Your Vision (Again)," Desiring God, November 16, 2011, https://www.desiringgod.org/articles/leaders-articulate-your-vision-again.

10. Proverbs 29:18 kjv.

Chapter 5: Cultivate Trustworthiness

1. George P. Schultz, "Trust Is the Coin of the Realm," *Hoover Institution*, December 11, 2020, https://www.hoover.org/research/trust-coin-realm.

2. Schultz, "Trust Is the Coin of the Realm."

3. Lee Rainie, Scott Keeter, and Andrew Perrin, "Trust and Distrust in America," Pew Research Center, July 22, 2019, https://www.pewresearch.org/politics/2019/07/22/trust-and-distrust-in-america.

4. Rainie, Keeter, Perrin, "Trust and Distrust in America."

5. Rainie, Keeter, Perrin, "Trust and Distrust in America."

6. Rainie, Keeter, Perrin, "Trust and Distrust in America."

7. Rainie, Keeter, Perrin, "Trust and Distrust in America."

8. Stephen M. R. Covey, *The Speed of Trust: The One Thing That Changes Everything* (New York: Free Press, 2006), 5.

9. Covey, *The Speed of Trust*, 30.

10. Robert B. Tucker, *Innovation Is Everybody's Business: How to Make Yourself Indispensable in Today's Hypercompetitive World* (Hoboken, NJ: Wiley, 2010), 157.

11. R. Judson Carlberg, "Managing the Organization" in David S. Dockery, ed., *Christian Leadership Essentials: A Handbook for Managing Christian Organizations* (Nashville, TN: B&H Academic, 2011), 89.

12. Francis X. Frei and Anne Morriss, "Begin with Trust," *Harvard Business Review*, May-June 2020, https://hbr.org/2020/05/begin-with-trust.

13. Covey, *The Speed of Trust*.

14. Michael Holland, "Authentic Leadership Revealed," Leadwell. Today, July 25, 2017, https://www.bishophouse.com/shareable/quote -authentic-leadership-revealed.

15. Mark Leibovich, "Amid Debacle in Kabul, Rumsfeld Is Laid to Rest," *New York Times*, August 25, 2021.

Chapter 6: Cherish Your Team

1. Jim Collins, *Good to Great: Why Some Companies Make the Leap and Others Don't* (New York: Harper Business, 2001).

Chapter 7: Insist on Accountability

1. Donald Rumsfeld, *Rumsfeld's Rules* (New York: HarperCollins Publishers, 2013), 220.

2. R. Albert Mohler, *The Conviction to Lead: 25 Principles for Leadership That Matters* (Minneapolis, MN: Bethany House, 2012), 112–13.

3. Rumsfeld, *Rumsfeld's Rules*, 87.

4. Patrick Lencioni, *The Advantage: Why Organizational Health Trumps Everything Else in Business*, 1st ed. (San Francisco: Jossey-Bass, 2012), 54–55.

5. Jon Wallace, "Financial Oversight and Budget Planning," in David S. Dockery, ed., *Christian Leadership Essentials: A Handbook for Managing Christian Organizations* (Nashville, TN: B&H Academic, 2011), 114.

6. Wallace, "Financial Oversight and Budget Planning," 106.

7. Wallace, "Financial Oversight and Budget Planning," 110.

8. J. Oswald Sanders, *Spiritual Leadership: Principles of Excellence for Every Believer*, updated ed. (Chicago, IL: Moody Publishers, 2007), 41.

Chapter 9: Communicate Clearly

1. Franklin D. Roosevelt, "Speech by Franklin D. Roosevelt, New York (Transcript)," loc.gov, Library of Congress, 1941, https://www.loc.gov /resource/afc1986022.afc1986022_ms2201/?st=text.

2. John F. Kennedy, "Inaugural Address of John F. Kennedy," avalon. law.yale.edu, Yale Law School Lillian Goldman Law Library, 1961, https:// avalon.law.yale.edu/20th_century/kennedy.asp.

3. Winston Churchill, "Blood, Toil, Tears and Sweat," International Churchill Society, May 13, 1940, https://winstonchurchill.org/resources /speeches/1940-the-finest-hour/blood-toil-tears-sweat.

4. Churchill, "Blood, Toil, Tears and Sweat."

5. Winston Churchill, "Speech before Commons," June 4, 1940, https:// history.hanover.edu/courses/excerpts/111chur.html.

6. Churchill, "Speech before Commons."

7. Winston Churchill, "The Finest Hour," International Churchill Society, 1940, https://winstonchurchill.org/resources/speeches/1940-the -finest-hour/their-finest-hour.

8. Edward R. Murrow, History Net, 1945, https://www.historynet.com/ photos-of-winston-churchill-at-war.htm/winston.

9. Chris Voss, *Never Split the Difference: Negotiating as if Your Life Depends on It* (New York: Harper Business, 2016).

10. Voss, *Never Split the Difference: Negotiating as if Your Life Depends on It*.

11. Hans Finzel, *The Top Ten Mistakes Leaders Make*, 2nd ed. (Colorado Springs, CO: David C. Cook, 2007), 135.

12. Finzel, *The Top Ten Mistakes Leaders Make*, 127.

13. Winston Churchill, "The Defence of Freedom and Peace (The Lights Are Going Out)," International Churchill Society, https://winston churchill.org/resources/speeches/1930-1938-the-wilderness/the-defence -of-freedom-and-peace-the-lights-are-going-out.

Chapter 10: Foster the Right Culture

1. Hans Finzel, *The Top Ten Mistakes Leaders Make*, 2nd ed. (Colorado Springs, CO: David C. Cook, 2007), 150.

2. Ralph Kilmann, *Beyond the Quick Fix: Managing Five Tracks to Organizational Success* (Fairless Hills, PA: Beard, 2004), 92.

3. Alan Kohll, "How to Build a Positive Company Culture," *Forbes*, August 14, 2018, https://www.forbes.com/sites/alankohll/2018/08/14/how-to-build-a-positive-company-culture/?sh=511f789249b5.

4. Patrick Lencioni, *The Advantage: Why Organizational Health Trumps Everything Else in Business*, 1st ed. (San Francisco: Jossey-Bass, 2012), 1.

5. Lencioni, *The Advantage*, 8.

6. Lencioni, *The Advantage*, 13.

7. Prasanna Singaraju, "Organizational Culture Is an Overlooked Factor in Transformation," *Forbes*, August 31, 2021, https://www.forbes.com/sites/forbestechcouncil/2021/08/31/organizational-culture-is-an-overlooked-factor-in-transformation/?sh=6517b6736420.

8. Lencioni, *The Advantage*, 5.

9. Philip W. Eaton, "Employee Relations in a Grace-Filled Community," in David S. Dockery, ed., *Christian Leadership Essentials: A Handbook for Managing Christian Organizations* (Nashville, TN: B&H Academic, 2011), 241.

Conclusion

1. Karen Zraick and Heather Murphy, "Notre-Dame Cathedral: Facts and a Brief History," *New York Times*, April 15, 2019, https://www.nytimes.com/2019/04/15/world/europe/notre-dame-cathedral-facts.html.

2. Blair Kamin, "Having Survived a Devastating Fire, the Heavenly Structure of Notre Dame Confronts Earthly Laws of Physics," *Chicago Tribune*, April 16, 2019, https://www.chicagotribune.com/columns/blair-kamin/ct-biz-notre-dame-structure-kamin-0416-story.html.